Photoshop® CS2 KillerTips

Scott Kelby • Felix Nelson

PHOTOSHOP® CS2 KILLER TIPS

The Photoshop® CS2
Killer Tips Team

TECHNICAL EDITORS
Polly Reincheld
Veronica Martin
Cindy Snyder

PRODUCTION EDITOR
Kim Gabriel

PRODUCTION MANAGER
Dave Damstra

COVER DESIGN AND
CREATIVE CONCEPTS
Felix Nelson

PUBLISHED BY
New Riders

Copyright © 2006 by Scott Kelby

FIRST EDITION: October 2005

Composed in Myriad Pro and Helvetica by NAPP Publishing

Trademarks
All terms mentioned in this book that are known to be trademarks or service marks have been appropriately capitalized. New Riders cannot attest to the accuracy of this information. Use of a term in the book should not be regarded as affecting the validity of any trademark or service mark.

Photoshop is a registered trademark of Adobe Systems, Inc.
Windows is a registered trademark of Microsoft Corporation.

Warning and Disclaimer
This book is designed to provide information about Photoshop tips. Every effort has been made to make this book as complete and as accurate as possible, but no warranty of fitness is implied.

The information is provided on an as-is basis. The authors and New Riders shall have neither liability nor responsibility to any person or entity with respect to any loss or damages arising from the information contained in this book or from the use of the discs or programs that may accompany it.

ISBN 0-321-33063-3

9 8 7 6 5 4 3 2 1

Printed in the United States of America

www.newriders.com
www.scottkelbybooks.com

ACKNOWLEDGMENTS

The downside of being a co-author is you only get half as much space to thank all of the wonderful people without whom you couldn't do any of this.

First, I want to thank my incredible wife Kalebra. I don't know what she puts in her morning coffee, but it must be working. Every year she gets more amazing, more beautiful, more hilarious, more savvy, and more just plain wonderful. She's my best friend, confidante, advice desk, gourmet chef, favorite artist, and the ultimate business partner. Best of all, she's a world-class mom, and it's an absolute joy seeing her special gifts reflected in our son Jordan. He has no idea how blessed and supremely lucky we both are to have her.

I want to thank my co-author, Felix Nelson, for agreeing to do this book with me. He's an amazing person—a great artist, with seemingly limitless enthusiasm and energy that has him perpetually in a good mood seven days a week.

His combination of talent, business savvy, and humor make him an absolute pleasure to work with, and I continue to learn more from him every day. I want to thank my world class Tech Editor Polly Reincheld for all her hard work and dedication, and thanks to my Production Editor Kim Gabriel for once again bringing the whole project together.

Thanks to Dave Cross and Matt Kloskowski for always sharing their favorite Photoshop tips with me, so I can pass them along to my readers, and thanks to best buddy Dave "Hey You!" Moser for kickin' so much butt out there.

I also want to thank my good friend and business partner Jean A. Kendra for all her support and enthusiasm for my projects. Special thanks to my brother Jeff for everything he does and for being such an important influence in my life. I want to thank everyone at KW Media Group who every day redefine what teamwork and dedication are all about. An extra special thanks to Kathy Siler for the hundreds of things she does that make my life and my work so much easier.

Thanks to Nancy Ruenzel, Scott Cowlin, Rachel Tiley and the entire crew at Peachpit for their commitment to excellence, and for the honor of letting me be one of their "Voices That Matter."

And most importantly, an extra special thanks to God and his son Jesus Christ for always hearing my prayers, for always being there when I need Him, and for blessing me with a life I truly love, and such a warm loving family to share it with.

—*SCOTT KELBY*

First, I'd like to thank my wife Patty, who is the kindest, most understanding and caring person on the face of the planet. Her positive outlook on life, no matter how chaotic the world is around her, is remarkable. A smile from her face can light up an entire room. Then there are my three sons, Earl, Chris, and Alex. Earl is the ultimate in cool. Nothing ever ruffles his feathers. To watch an adorable, curly-headed little boy grow up into such a wonderful young man has been my greatest source of pride. And Chris "the studier" is the hardest-working, nose-to-the-grindstone person you'd ever want to meet. His drive and determination astonishes me. He's just a fantastic kid. Then there's little Alex. It's absolutely amazing how this little person affects my life. No matter how bad or how stressful the day has been, a hug from those tiny little arms and an "I love you Daddy" from those big brown eyes just melt my heart. He makes me realize things are never quite as bad as they appear.

My involvement in this book would not have been possible without the guidance and tutelage of Scott Kelby. He is without a doubt the most energetic, ambitious, and entertaining person I've ever met. His motor just never stops running. I can't begin to tell you how much he's influenced my life. He's a great mentor and a wonderful human being. I also have to thank the partners of KW Media Group (Jim Workman, Jean Kendra, and Kalebra Kelby) for the opportunities they've given me. When it comes to hard work and dedication, they're right up there with Scott. They're an amazing group and I'm a better person for knowing them.

Thanks to Dave Moser and Kim Gabriel who, come hell or high water, make sure the trains run on time. Of course, I can't forget about "Super Dave" Damstra, Dave "#5" Korman, Margie Rosenstien, Taffy Orlowski, and Christine Edwards who do the work of about 20 ordinary designers. They Rock. Thanks to Polly, Veronica, and Cindy, the tech editing "book babes". I'd also like to thank Chris Main and Barbara Thompson, Managing Editors extraordinaire, they could proofread an entire set of encyclopedias in an afternoon, and still have time for beer and a game of darts. And a special thanks to everyone else at KW Media Group, working behind the scenes, from the mailroom to customer service, who make us all look good.

—*FELIX NELSON*

ABOUT THE AUTHORS

Scott Kelby

Scott is Editor-in-Chief and co-founder of *Photoshop User* magazine, Editor-in-Chief of Nikon's *Capture User* magazine, Editor-in-Chief of *Layers* magazine (The How-To Magazine for Everything Adobe), and is Executive Editor of the *Photoshop Elements Techniques* newsletter.

He is President of the National Association of Photoshop Professionals (NAPP), the trade association for Adobe® Photoshop® users, and he's President of the software training and publishing firm, KW Media Group, Inc.

Scott is an award-winning author of more than 26 books on Photoshop, digital imaging, and technology. In 2004, he was the world's #1 bestselling author of all computer and technology books. His other titles include *Photoshop Down & Dirty Tricks, Photoshop Photo-Retouching Secrets, Photoshop Classic Effects, The Photoshop Elements Book for Digital Photographers,* and he's creator and series Editor for the entire *Killer Tips* series from New Riders.

Scott's latest books include *The iPod Book* and *The Book for Guys Who Don't Want Kids (How to Get Past the Fear of Fatherhood)*. In 2004, Scott was awarded the publishing industry's prestigious Benjamin Franklin Award for the previous edition of this book.

Scott is Training Director for the Adobe Photoshop Seminar Tour, Conference Technical Chair for the Photoshop World Conference & Expo, and he is a speaker at digital imaging trade shows and events around the world. He is also featured in a series of Adobe Photoshop training DVDs and has been training Adobe Photoshop users since 1993.

For more background info on Scott, visit www.scottkelby.com.

Felix Nelson

Felix Nelson is the Creative Director of *Photoshop User* magazine, the Senior Art Director for the National Association of Photoshop Professionals (NAPP), and the Art Director for *Layers* magazine, The How-To Magazine for Everything Adobe. Felix is a contributing author to *Photoshop Effects Magic* from New Riders and served as technical consultant for *Photoshop Down & Dirty Tricks.* Felix is also featured in a Photoshop training video, *Photoshop Photorealistic Techniques*, and is a member of the Photoshop World instructor "Dream Team."

He's a traditional illustrator who took a "digital-u-turn" in 1988 when he was first introduced to a Mac IIcx. His design work and digital illustrations have been featured on NBA-, NFL-, and MLB-licensed sports apparel and have appeared in several national publications.

Felix lives in Spring Hill, Florida, with his wife Patty and sons Alex, Chris, and Earl.

TABLE OF CONTENTS

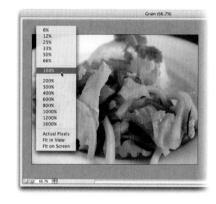

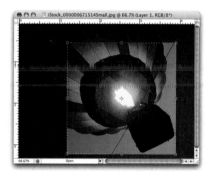

TABLE OF CONTENTS

TABLE OF CONTENTS

CHAPTER 7   147
Burn Rubber
Smokin' Type Tips

TABLE OF CONTENTS

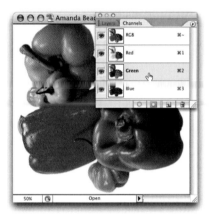

TABLE OF CONTENTS

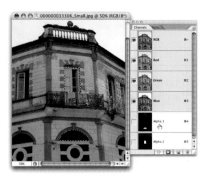

INTRODUCTION

Why we wrote this book

The inspiration for this book came when Felix saw what the car payment would be on a new Porsche Boxster. He came to me and said, "Dude, I gotta write a book." Okay, you know we're kidding, but admit it—don't you secretly wish that for once, when someone was doing something strictly for the money, they'd just come out and say so. Just once, wouldn't you like to hear someone admit it? Well, I hate to disappoint you, but I can tell you unequivocally that Felix and I absolutely did not write this book for the money. We wrote it to get free drugs. All authors get free drugs—it's in every book contract. Always has been.

Actually, the reason we wanted to write this book is because of something that is already in almost every Photoshop book ever written: the tips. You know—those cool little tips littered throughout the sidebars of all great Photoshop books. We found that those little tips were often our favorite parts of the book. In fact, Felix and I agreed that frequently we'd read all those little sidebar tips first—before we'd ever sit down to actually read a chapter. It's those neat little tips that the great authors include that make using Photoshop so much fun (and make their books so great). The only problem is, there's just not enough of 'em.

So we thought, "Wouldn't it be cool if there was a Photoshop book where the whole book, cover-to-cover, was nothing but those little tips on the side!" Then Felix jumped up and yelled, "Let's write that book!" I jumped up and yelled, "Yes, yes! We have to write that book. It's our destiny!" Then Felix yelled, "Then I can get my Porsche!" I mean, he yelled, "This book will help humanity and be written for the common good" (or something like that. I can't remember. Probably because of all the drugs).

Is this book for you?

Is this book for you? Are you kidding? This book is so for you that it secretly freaks you out. Look, we don't know you personally, but we know Photoshop people. You're just like us—you love those little sidebar tips just as much as we do. If you didn't, authors would've stopped adding them to their books years ago, because, frankly, they're a pain in the butt to compile. But we know what you're thinking. Sure, you love those little tips—those inside secrets that make you look smart at parties and gain respect from your peers, homies, peeps, and other esteemed colleagues, but you want something more. You want the one thing that those cool little sidebar tips never seem to have. That's right, graphics. As cool as those sidebar tips are, they're always just a tiny little box with a couple of lines of text (like the sidebar we added above left). So we thought we'd expand the explanations just enough to make them more accessible, and add an accompanying graphic to enhance each tip's innate juiciness. They must remain "juicy." They must be "juicy tips."

Now you're probably wondering, "Guys, Photoshop is one amazing program with an unrivaled power and incredible depth. Couldn't you have come up with at least 1,000 Photoshop tips?" Absolutely. We could have included loads of tips, such as "F7 brings up the Layers palette," and "Press G-Shift-G to get the Paint Bucket tool," but the problem is, those aren't "Killer Tips." Every Photoshop book has those tips. Heck, books about gardening probably even have those Photoshop tips. For a tip to get in this book, it had to be a "Killer Tip." Each tip had to be one that would make the reader smile, nod, and then pick up the phone to call another Photoshop user just to "tune them up" with their newfound power. Remember, these are killer tips, so be careful. Someone could get hurt.

TIP

This is a sidebar tip. Every great Photoshop book has a few of them. But this book is nothing but them. A whole book of cool sidebar tips, without the sidebars.

Okay, how do I get started?

In my previous Photoshop books, *Photoshop CS Down & Dirty Tricks* and *The Photoshop CS2 Book for Digital Photographers*, I used a technique that really worked well. I gratuitously mentioned my other books in the introduction, just in case I didn't get to plug them later. No, wait… that's not it. What I did tell the reader was that my books aren't set up like a novel. They're purposely not designed to make you start at Chapter One and read your way through to the back (where hopefully, I'll again have an opportunity to plug, I mean casually mention, my other books). Instead, this book is designed so you can jump in anywhere, in any chapter, and immediately try the tips that interest you the most, regardless of your level of experience in Photoshop. You don't need to load any special images from a CD-ROM or go to a website to download special photos—these are just cool tips. No flaming type, no multilevel glows—just timesaving shortcuts and efficiency tips that will make you faster and better at Photoshop than you'd ever thought you'd be.

Also, like my previous books, we spell out everything. So if you've been using Photoshop for years, don't let it frustrate you because instead of just writing, "Create a new layer," we usually write, "Create a new layer by clicking on the New Layer icon at the bottom of the Layers palette." We do that because we want everyone, at any skill level, to be able to open the book to any page and start applying these cool tips to their work immediately.

This book is built on the premise that "Speed Kills." Because after all, if you get faster at Photoshop, you'll have more time to be creative, and the more time you spend being creative, the more fun you'll have.

Is this book for Macintosh, Windows, or both?

This book is not only for Mac and Windows users, it's for people who don't even have a computer. In fact, it's ideal for anyone with $29.99 (kidding). Because Photoshop is identical on both the Macintosh and Windows operating systems, the book is for both Mac and Windows users. However, the keyboards on a Mac and PC are slightly different, so every time we give a keyboard shortcut, we give both the Mac and Windows shortcuts. (Well, there is one other difference—in Mac OS X you'll find Photoshop's Preferences under the Photoshop menu instead of the Edit menu like it used to be in the Mac OS and still is in Windows.)

How to use this book

This book is designed to be read while moving at a high rate of speed. If you're barreling down the highway going 80 mph, weaving in and out of traffic, that's the ideal time to turn to Chapter Six to read the tip on "How to assist EMS workers with using the Jaws of Life." Okay, admittedly, that's probably not a good idea, so instead, just make sure you open this book in front of your computer so you can dive right into the tips. Remember, the one who dies with the most cool tips wins.

What not to do

You're almost ready to get to the tips, but first a word of caution: "Caution." There. Now you're ready. Actually, we did want to point out that the only two actual sidebar tips in the entire book are on these two pages. So, don't go rippin' through the book looking for all those little sidebar tips, because we intentionally left the sidebars blank. Why? So we could write another book called *The Missing Killer Tips Sidebars*, just in case Felix ever sees what the payment is for a house on the beach.

TIP

You're doing it again! Stop looking at these sidebars. See, they're intoxicating—you're drawn to them even after you know it's not really a tip. Okay, here's a real tip: If you like sidebar tips, buy this book.

These chapter intros are usually Scott's area of expertise, but when we decided to add Adobe Bridge killer tips to this book, I felt the need to purge myself and release some inner

Speed Ballin'
adobe bridge tips

demons. Now, I don't have a problem with the Bridge software. Not at all, I love Bridge. And it isn't a fear of actual bridges, too. I dig real bridges, too. It's the word "bridge" itself that has blackened my heart. Even worse, Clint Eastwood, one of my favorite actors of all time, is forever linked to this vile and venomous word.

What created this inner turmoil? What horrific event triggered this kind of repulsive response to a simple word, you ask? The Bridges of Madison County, *that's what. Watching that one movie tainted the word bridge forever. There I was, waiting to hear Dirty Harry utter one of those famous one-liners—"Go ahead, make my day" or "Do you feel lucky punk?" Heck, simply hearing Philo Beddoe say "Right turn, Clyde" just one time could have saved the show. But nope, it wasn't to be. There he was, the outlaw Josey Wales, in a chick flick. Not just a chick flick, but maybe one of the worst films ever documented.*

But hey, that was a long time ago. Maybe I should just let it go and forget about the past. Clint's new movie, Million Dollar Baby, *is getting a lot of good press. I mean, it is Clint Eastwood after all, and it's about boxing. That's got machismo written all over it. Right?*

UNDOCUMENTED BRIDGE SLIDE SHOW TIP

Here's one that slipped below the radar—if you're watching a slide show of your images in Bridge (by pressing Command-L [PC: Control-L]), and you come across an image you want to open in Photoshop CS2, just press the letter O.

SCROLLING THROUGH THE VIEWS

Want to quickly scroll through the different thumbnail views in Bridge? Press-and-hold Command (PC: Control) and the Backslash key (\). Hey, don't scoff at this seemingly innocent shortcut—Mac users have been waiting years for any shortcut that makes use of the Backslash key. In the captures shown here, I've scrolled from Thumbnails view to Filmstrip view.

OPEN ANY FOLDER WITH A SIMPLE DRAG-AND-DROP

Want to open a folder of images in Bridge? Just drag-and-drop the folder directly onto the Preview panel. That's it. I wish this tip were longer, but it's just not.

RATING MULTIPLE PHOTOS AT ONCE

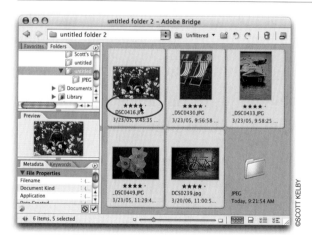

If you see a number of photos in Bridge that you want to have the same rating, first select the images (Shift-click on them or Command-click [PC: Control-click] noncontiguous images), then drag your cursor over the rating area (those five dots that appear below any selected thumbnail). The rating you apply to that one photo will be applied to all your selected photos.

CREATING NEW FOLDERS THE FAST WAY

Want to create a folder from right within Bridge? Scroll down to any open space (you'll usually find a blank spot at the bottom of your list of thumbnails, so scroll down there), then Control-click (PC: Right-click) and from the contextual menu that appears, choose New Folder. *Note:* If you don't see any empty space, adjust the size of your images using the Thumbnail Size slider along the bottom of the Bridge window.

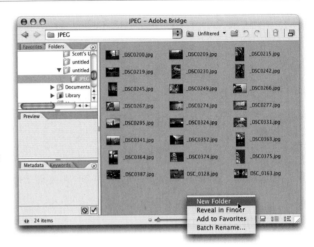

SEPARATING YOUR "BEST OF THE BEST"

If you've rated some of your photos as five-star photos (the best of the bunch), aren't there some five-star photos that are better than the others? You know, the best of your best? Of course there are, and now you can separate just those (so you can really see the cream of the crop). Here's how: First you must view just your five-star photos, so choose Show 5 Stars from the Unfiltered pop-up menu near the top right of the Options Bar. Then Command-click (PC: Control-click) on just your best

five-star images to select them. Control-click (PC: Right-click) on any selected image and choose a color from the Label submenu in the contextual menu that appears (I chose Red). That color is now tagging your best five-star images. To see just your red five-star photos, go back to the Filtered pop-up menu (it'll change from Unfiltered to Filtered once you've selected an option), and choose Show Red Label. Now you're seeing your "Best of the Best."

©SCOTT KELBY

RATING YOUR IMAGES IN FULL SCREEN MODE

This is one of the most effective ways to sort your photos after you've imported them from your digital camera, because you can only really tell which photos are in sharp focus when they're viewed at nearly full screen. So in Bridge, Shift-click on all the contiguous photos you want to review, press Command-L (PC: Control-L) to launch the slide show, press W to see the images full screen, and then press Spacebar to start the slide show. As a photo appears full screen, just press numbers (1–5) to rate that photo instantly. For example, a photo appears onscreen and it's not that great, type 3 and it gets a three-star rating right on the spot. Try this once, and you'll start doing this all the time. Unless of course, you hate it—then you'll probably never do it again.

A SNEAK PEEK AT YOUR PHOTO'S DATA

You don't have to go digging through your photo's EXIF data to learn more about the image. Just hover your cursor over a photo's thumbnail for a moment, and a little yellow window will pop up with some brief background info, like the file's format, size, pixel dimensions, date created, date modified, resolution, etc. However, this only works if you have Tooltips turned on, so if you don't, press Command-K (PC: Control-K) to open the Bridge Preferences, choose General (from the left side of the dialog), and turn on the checkbox for Show Tooltips; now try the hovering trick again.

⬤ ⬤ ⬤ UNCLUTTERING YOUR VIEW

Want to hide all of that distracting info that appears beneath your
thumbnails? Just press Command-T
(PC: Control-T) and all that stuff (even
the file names) is hidden, giving you a
clean, unobstructed view of just your
images and nothing more. When you
want all the distracting junk back, just
press the shortcut again.

⬤ ⬤ ⬤ RENAMING YOUR LABEL COLORS

Although you can't change the color of the color labels themselves, you can change each
color's name to something that makes more sense to you when you're sorting your images.
For example, if you want change the Green label to read "Keepers," just press Command-K
(PC: Control-K) to go to the Bridge Preferences, click on Labels (along the list on the left
side of the dialog), and then delete the word "Green" that appears to the right of the green
dot and type "Keepers." Click OK to close the Preferences dialog. Now, when you look in the
Label menu, it will be updated with your new name.

⬤ ⬤ ⬤ KEEPING BRIDGE ALWAYS ON TOP

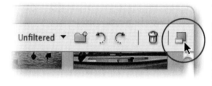

The idea behind Bridge is to use it to manage all your images for all your programs, and if you're doing just that, you'll definitely want to know how to keep Bridge up front and floating above whichever program you currently have open. First, click on the Switch to Compact Mode icon that appears in the upper-right corner of Bridge's Options Bar. Then, once it switches to Compact Mode, a new icon will now appear to the left of that icon—the Switch to Ultra-Compact Mode icon (I kid you not). If you use either Compact Mode, Bridge will remain at the foreground just like a floating palette, no matter which program you're using. To stop the floating, just click on the Switch to Full Mode icon (which had been the Compact Mode icon—it changes its function depending on the mode you're using—I know, it's confusing).

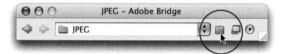

⬤ ⬤ ⬤ RESETTING BRIDGE'S PREFERENCES

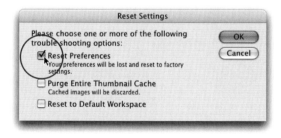

Want all the options in Bridge set back to the factory defaults? Then close Bridge, hold down Command-Option-Shift (PC: Control-Alt-Shift), and then launch Bridge again. A dialog will appear asking what you want to do. Turn on the Reset Preferences checkbox and click OK. Now when Bridge appears, the preferences are factory-fresh.

DELETING FOLDERS FROM BRIDGE

This is one Adobe snuck into CS2, and they made so little fuss about it, hardly anyone realizes they did it—you can now delete entire folders right within Bridge. Just click on the folder and press Command-Delete (PC: Control-Delete). Now, with great power comes great responsibility, so don't just start deleting stuff all willy-nilly (by the way, I have no idea what willy-nilly means), because those folders have photos in 'em. Even though you'll get a warning dialog before the folder disappears, make sure that before you click OK to delete a folder, that's really what you want to do.

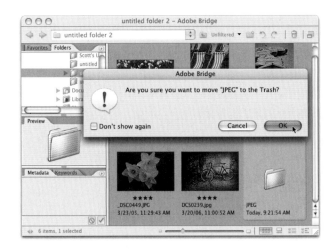

SEEING MORE THAN ONE FOLDER OF IMAGES AT A TIME

If you'd like to see more than one folder of photos onscreen at the same time, it's no problem, because in CS2 you can have multiple Bridge windows open at the same time. Just press Command-N (PC: Control-N) and a new Bridge window will appear (your previous Bridge window will still be there). Now, navigate to the folder you want to display in this window, and you're set—your original window is still open, and your new window is showing some new photos. Mighty darn handy stuff for a Buckaroo like yourself.

©SCOTT KELBY

VIEWING THE PAGES OF PDFS FROM WITHIN BRIDGE

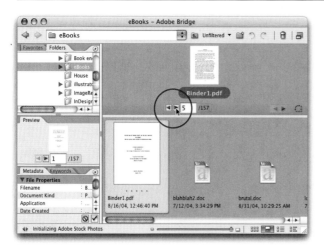

Got a multipage PDF and want to see inside it? No sweat—just switch to Filmstrip view (click the Filmstrip icon near the bottom-right corner of the Bridge window), click on the PDF's thumbnail in Bridge, and little arrow buttons will appear beneath the PDF, which let you move from page to page inside the PDF.

SEEING YOUR PDF PAGES BIGGER

If you're using the previous tip to view PDF documents within Bridge, here's a tip you'll probably want to know to make your PDF's pages appear larger onscreen. If your PDF contains regular letter-sized pages, click the Switch Filmstrip Orientation icon found to the right of the arrow buttons below the PDF. This switches your view so your thumbnails appear along the side, which makes your letter-sized pages larger. Now you can grab the bottom-right corner of the Bridge window and expand it to make your view even bigger, so it's "biggity big" (that's a technical term, not to be used lightly).

HOW TO GET MORE THAN THREE PANES

That headline is a setup I can hardly resist, but I'm going to totally ignore it and jump right to the tip, although it panes me. (Sorry, I couldn't help it.) By default, Bridge (and the File Browsers that came before it) has three panes visible on the left side of the window (with the Folders and Favorites panels on top, Preview in the middle, and the Metadata and Keywords panels below that). But in CS2 it doesn't have to be just three—you can add more panes (ideal if you're working on a really large monitor). Here's how: Just click-and-drag the tab of the pane you want to have in its own section until it appears right beneath one of the existing panes. When you see a thick, blue horizontal line appear between the two panes, that's your cue—release the mouse button, and your pane has a new home.

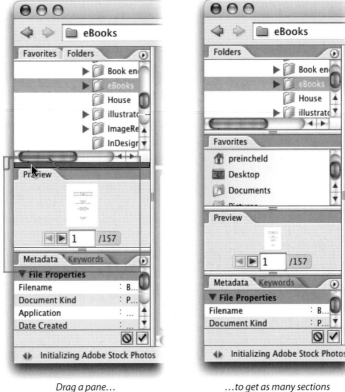

Drag a pane…   *…to get as many sections as you'd like.*

HOW TO KNOW IF A PHOTO IS OPEN IN PHOTOSHOP

If you're in Bridge and notice a little round icon with a bent page has appeared in the bottom-right corner of your thumbnail, that's Bridge's way of telling you that the image is currently open in Photoshop.

OPENING AN IMAGE AND HIDING YOUR BRIDGE WINDOW

One thing that really adds to your desktop clutter is the fact that when you open a photo from Bridge, your Bridge window remains open behind your photo. In most cases, you can still see the top, right-hand side, bottom, or all sides (depending on the size of your image) peeking out from behind your photo. But it doesn't have to be that way. To open a photo and have Bridge automatically close its window, don't just double-click on the thumbnail to open it; instead, Option-double-click (PC: Alt-double-click) on the thumbnail.

I WANNA GO BACK

If you're on a webpage and you want to go back to the previous page, you just hit the Back button, right? Well, luckily Adobe added a Back button to Bridge as well, so to get back to your previous folder of images, just click the Go Back button (it's the left-facing arrow) at the top-left corner of your Bridge window. You can also go to your next folder by clicking the Go Forward button (it's the right-facing arrow), but did I really have to tell you that?

FASTER COLOR LABELING SHORTCUT

By default, the shortcuts for applying a color label require you to hold down the Command key (PC: Control key), so you'd press Command-6 for Red, Command-7 for Yellow, etc. (PC: Control-6, -7, etc.). But if you find yourself using color labels a lot, you can change it so it only takes one key—the number, rather than Command/Control. Just press Command-K (PC: Control-K) to go to the Bridge Preferences, click on Labels (from the list on the left side of the dialog), and then turn off the checkbox for Require the Command Key (PC: Control Key) to Apply Labels and Ratings.

GETTING BACK TO YOUR BRIDGE WINDOW AFTER SEARCHING

When you perform a search (by pressing Command-F [PC: Control-F]), although it at first seems that your results appear within your same Bridge window—they don't. They appear in their own separate window, so if you want to get back to working in Bridge, you have to close the results window.

COLLECTIONS ARE LIVE, BABY!

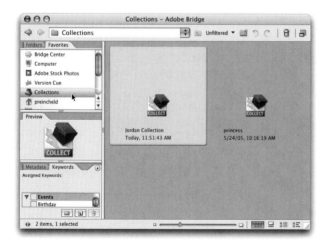

If you create a collection (let's say it's a collection of all photos on your hard disk that have your son's or daughter's name as the keyword), this collection is "live" and by that I mean that anytime you import a new photo and assign that same keyword (your son's or daughter's name), that photo will automatically also appear in that collection (well, technically it updates the next time you click on that collection, but that's technical, right?). To create a collection, just do a search for the keyword you want by pressing Command-F (PC: Control-F), enter your criteria in the Find dialog, and then once the results window appears, click on the Save As Collection button in the top-right corner. To see if your imported image appeared in your collection, click on Collections in the Favorites pane, and double-click on the collection to open it in its own window.

● ● ● DUPLICATE ANY PHOTO FAST!

Want to duplicate an image in Bridge? Just click on it and press Command-D (PC: Control-D) and it will appear at the bottom of your Bridge window. This used to be the shortcut for Deselect All back in the File Browser of CS, but now it duplicates the image. That's probably got you thinking, "Hey, so if Command-D doesn't deselect all, what shortcut does?" It's Command-Shift-A (PC: Control-Shift-A).

● ● ● DELETING UNWANTED PHOTOS FAST

Let's say you've opened the photos from your latest shoot (after you've backed them up to CD, of course), and you realize there are only five or six photos that you really want to keep, and you want to delete the rest. Use this tip to make quick work of getting rid of the hundreds you don't want—just Command-click (PC: Control-click) on the five or six you want to keep, then go under the Edit menu and choose Invert Selection. This command selects every photo *but* those five or six you selected. Now you can just press Command-Delete (PC: Control-Delete) to delete all the ones you don't want. Big time saver.

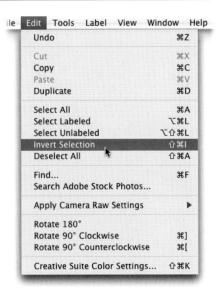

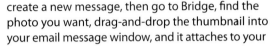
● ● ● EMAILING FROM BRIDGE

Okay, you can't exactly email from Bridge, but this is the closest thing—you can drag images directly from Bridge right into your email message window. Just open your email program, create a new message, then go to Bridge, find the photo you want, drag-and-drop the thumbnail into your email message window, and it attaches to your message. *Note:* This can vary depending on the email program you use.

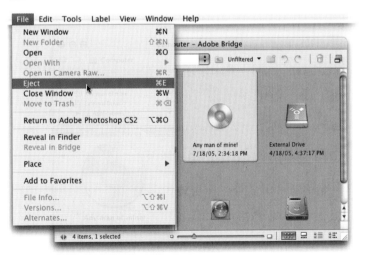

● ● ● EJECTING DISCS FROM WITHIN BRIDGE

If you've got a CD, jump drive, a camera memory card, etc., hooked up to your computer, you can eject it without leaving Bridge. Just go to the Folders pane, click on the disc you want to eject, then go under Bridge's File menu and choose Eject.

RENAME ANY PHOTO FAST

Want to rename a photo? Just click on its thumbnail then press the Spacebar. Its name will highlight and you can just type in a new one. When you're done, just press the Enter key.

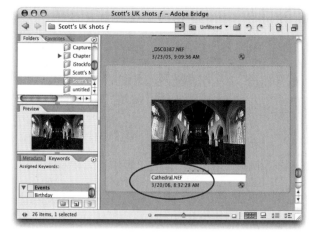

SWITCHING BETWEEN OPEN BRIDGE WINDOWS

As you learned earlier, you can have more than one Bridge window open at a time (which is great for looking at different collections of images at the same time). Well, if you're going to be working with multiple windows, you're going to want to know this shortcut, which toggles you back and forth between open Bridge windows. It's Command-Shift-~ (that's the Tilde key, found right above the Tab key on your keyboard). *Note:* Unfortunately for PC users, this shortcut doesn't work.

JUMP TO THE LARGEST THUMBNAIL SIZE IN ONE CLICK

If you want to see your thumbnails as large as they can possibly fit within Bridge's main window, just go down to the Thumbnail Size slider (along the bottom of the window) and click on the little rectangle icon that appears at the end of the slider on the right side. This jumps you instantly to the largest possible thumbnail size in just one click.

HOW TO KEEP FROM LOSING YOUR BRIDGE CHANGES

Before there was Bridge, there was the File Browser. One downfall of the File Browser was that if you moved photos from one folder to another, you lost all the changes (and cached thumbnails) you had made while in the Browser because you lost the link to the invisible files that stored that information. But you can change that in Bridge, so your edits (and thumbnail cache) follow wherever you move your folder of images. First, press Command-K (PC: Control-K) to bring up Bridge's Preferences. On the left side of the dialog, click on Advanced, and then click on the Use Distributed Cache Files When Possible option under the Cache section. This makes two normally invisible files now visible, and when you move your folder of images, they move right along with them.

 **BATCH RENAMING EARNS A SHORTCUT**

Finally, the Batch Rename command (where you rename multiple photos at once) has a keyboard shortcut. It's Command-Shift-R (PC: Control-Shift-R), which brings up the Batch Rename dialog (as shown here).

 **JUMPING BETWEEN BRIDGE AND PHOTOSHOP**

Here's a shortcut you'll want to start using to jump you back and forth between Photoshop and Bridge (when they're both already open). It's Command-Option-O (PC: Control-Alt-O).

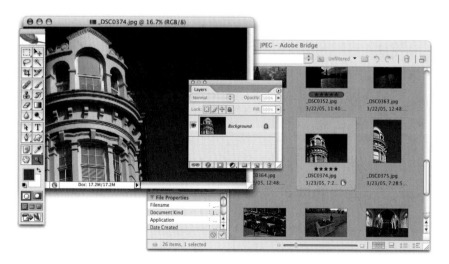

ONE-BUTTON REFRESH FOR BRIDGE

When you're working in CS2's Bridge, you've probably noticed that when you plug in a jump drive, memory card, etc., your Folders pane doesn't always update immediately. If that's the case, there's a simple one-button trick—press F5. If you're charging by the hour, you could always choose Refresh from the Folders palette's flyout menu, but that just takes too long. Instead, just press F5 for an instant refresh anytime.

CHANGING METADATA FONT SIZES

If you're older than 17, chances are you'll find the font size Adobe uses for the Metadata palette in Bridge way, way too small. Luckily, Adobe doesn't have many 17-year-olds on the payroll, so they included a way to increase the font size for the metadata. Just click on the flyout menu (it's the little round button with a right-facing triangle in it on the top-right side of the Metadata palette) and choose Increase Font Size from the contextual menu. The cool thing is—you can choose this command more than once, making your font size bigger and bigger each time you choose it.

⬤ ⬤ ⬤ NESTING YOUR BRIDGE PANES

Nesting palettes (putting commonly used palettes together in one palette, with just their tabs showing) is very popular in Photoshop, and you're able to do that within Bridge as well. Just drag-and-drop the tab of one palette onto another palette (just like you would outside Bridge). For example, if you'd like all four Bridge pane tabs side-by-side at the top of the Bridge's Panel area, just drag the lower three tabs up to the Folders pane, one by one.

⬤ ⬤ ⬤ MAKING THE PREVIEW PALETTE BIGGER

Want a taller preview in Bridge for photos taken in a portrait orientation (tall rather than wide)? Just double-click on the Folders (or Favorites) tab, then double-click the Metadata (or Keywords) tab), and they will both "roll up," allowing the Preview pane to expand, giving you a preview that's twice as tall.

SAVING BRIDGE WORKSPACES

In Bridge, your custom setups can be saved as workspaces. For example, if you shoot a lot of portraits, you could use the previous tip to set up your Bridge window to your liking and then save it by going to the Window menu, under Workspace, and choosing Save Workspace (name it something you'll remember, like "Bridge Portrait"). Then, next time you're looking through some proofs, you can have huge previews in just one click. You can do the same thing for wide horizontal photos—just drag the divider bar along the Panel area to the right until the preview takes up most of the Bridge window. Now switching between huge portrait and landscape previews only takes one click.

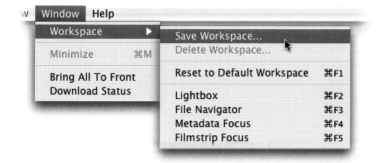

Have you ever been to one of those trendy Photoshop parties? You know the ones I mean—where the guests sit around in the study, ensconced in big leather chairs, smoking

Born to Run
essential tips you've got to know

smuggled Cuban cigars, and casually chatting about "calculating this and masking that…," and they keep referring to the time they were out on their yacht with Deke, Ben, and Jack. Don't you hate those parties? Me too. But nonetheless, I don't want to get caught at one of them and be the only goober there who didn't know that Shift-Delete is the undocumented shortcut for bringing up the Fill dialog. Imagine the shame. Then you'd have to pull that old, "Oh, I knew that, I thought you were referring to something in the Curves dialog that I heard at RIT," as they all slowly look away, rolling their eyes, glancing at each other with that "who's the spaz?" look on their faces. Do you want to be that person? Do you want to be that spaz? No? Then read this chapter, dammit. Memorize every word, every line, every keyboard shortcut. Then fire up a fat boy and head for the study. It's time to find a spaz to tease until he's in the fetal position.

FIND ALL THE NEW CS2 STUFF FAST!

Want to instantly find all the areas where Adobe added something new in CS2? Then go under the Window menu, under Workspace, and choose What's New in CS2. This is a custom workspace that puts a color bar over every menu item that has something new in it. For example, now when you look under the Filter menu, you'll see that the filter Vanishing Point is highlighted, as are the submenus Blur, Distort, Noise, and Sharpen. *Note:* When you choose this option, you will likely get a warning dialog telling you that this will change your work-space—just click Yes and enjoy the colorful menus.

THE MOST LONG-AWAITED SHORTCUT MAKES ITS DEBUT

If there was a keyboard shortcut that we've been waiting for since Photoshop 1.0, it was one for the Image Size dialog. It's one of the most-used dialogs in all of Photoshop, but there's never been a "factory" shortcut for it until now. Press Command-Option-I (PC: Control-Alt-I) and it pops up. Luckily, while Adobe was at it, they went ahead and gave us one for the Canvas Size dialog as well: Command-Option-C (PC: Control-Alt-C).

CURSOR TOO SMALL? MAKE IT BIGGER

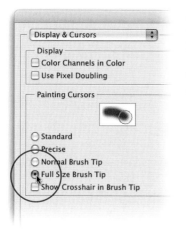

At long last, bigger brush cursors are here. Just go to Prefer-ences under the Photoshop menu (or under the Edit menu in Windows), under Display & Cursors, and choose Full Size Brush Tip. You also have the option of adding a crosshair to the center of your brush cursor by turning on that option (which appears just below Full Size Brush Tip).

SIDE-BY-SIDE PHOTO REVIEW

Want to compare two photos side-by-side? Just open both in Photoshop CS2, then go under the Window menu, under Arrange, and choose Tile Vertically, which places both photos onscreen, side-by-side, at their maximum "fit-in-window" size.

©ISTOCKPHOTO/AMANDA ROHDE

WANT SOME HINTS FOR THE TOOL YOU'RE CURRENTLY USING?

If you want some tips about the tool you currently have selected, just go to the Window menu and choose Info. This brings up the Info palette and at the bottom of the palette you'll find a tip or two for the tool you're using. If you don't see these tips, go to the Info palette's flyout menu and choose Palette Options. When the options appear, at the bottom turn on the checkbox for Show Tool Hints.

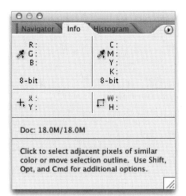

DON'T USE IT? HIDE IT!

Photoshop has more than a hundred different filters, and most of us probably use just a handful in our daily work. In fact, so far as we've been able to determine (through years of user-testing), only three people in the world today use either the Pattern Maker filter or the Fiber filter, and even they don't like them. So, if there are filters you never use, do they have to hang around clogging up your filter menus? Absolutely not (if you have CS2). Just go under the Edit menu and choose Menus. In the list of Application Menus commands, double-click on Filter to reveal a list of all Photoshop filters. Now, just turn off the Eye icon (a.k.a. the Visibility button) beside the filters you don't want to see. Don't worry, if for some reason you decide you need to temporarily access one of those hidden filters, just go under the Filter menu, to the submenu where it used to appear, and choose Show All Menu Items.

A TIP FOR PEOPLE WHO TRAIN NEW PHOTOSHOP USERS

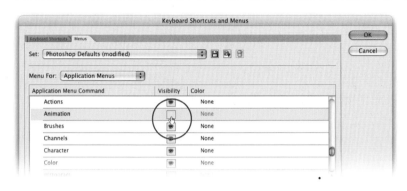

If you're responsible for training beginners, especially in a corporate environment where you're training people to do specific tasks in a specific order (like prepress), you can use this and the previous tip to make your (and their) life easier. First, go to the Menus command (found under the Edit menu) and hide every menu item you don't want them to see or mess with, leaving only the items they'll actually use visible. You can even hide palettes they don't need to see (by double-clicking on the word "Window" in the dialog and turning off the Eye icons to hide palettes). This makes Photoshop appear less cluttered, and therefore less intimidating. As they learn more and get better, you can reveal additional features to them.

LOST YOUR CURSOR? FIND IT FAST!

| Where's my cursor? | There it is. |

Photoshop's cursors can be easy to lose onscreen, especially if you're working on a big screen or with the crosshair cursor (meaning you have the Caps Lock key active). Well, the next time you're working on an image, and you say to yourself, "Hey, where in the heck is my cursor?" (but you use a different word in place of "heck"), try this—just hold the Spacebar down for a moment. This temporarily changes your cursor into the Hand tool, whose icon is larger, white, and easy to see. Once it appears, you'll see right where your cursor is, and you can release the Spacebar.

● ● ● THE HIDDEN MEASUREMENT POP-UP MENU

You probably already know the trick about entering values in measurement fields in the Options Bar. You can change your unit of measure by typing the appropriate abbreviation after the value (for example, if you want 100 pixels, you'd type in "100 px"). But there's an even easier way (and you don't have to memorize a bunch of abbreviations). Just type your number, Control-click (PC: Right-click) in the field, and a pop-up menu of measurement units will appear. Just choose the one you want and it'll take care of the rest.

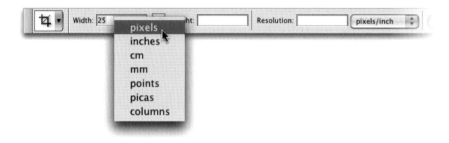

● ● ● GETTING A FRESH HISTOGRAM IN ONE CLICK

When you have the Histogram palette open to monitor your tonal adjustments to an image, you may see a tiny warning symbol in the top-right corner of your histogram. That's its way of letting you know that you're looking at a histogram reading from the histogram's memory cache—not a fresh reading. If you want to refresh the histogram and get a new reading (and you should), you can click directly on the tiny warning symbol and it will refresh immediately for you.

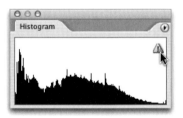

USING THE LASSO TOOL? KEEP IT STRAIGHT

We normally use the Lasso tool (L) for drawing freeform selections, but sometimes you'll find that while drawing your selection you'll need to draw a perfectly straight segment, even for just a few pixels. You can do just that by holding the Option key (PC: Alt key), releasing the mouse button, and continuing to draw your selection. You'll notice that your cursor changes to the Polygonal Lasso tool, and that as you move the mouse, a perfectly straight selection will drag out. When you've dragged the straight selection where you want, click-and-hold the mouse button (to add a point), release the Option/Alt key, and you'll be back to the regular Lasso tool again. Drag the mouse to continue drawing your selection.

CAN'T REMEMBER SELECTION SHORTCUTS? LOOK AT THE CURSOR

If you've made a selection and want to add to that selection, just hold the Shift key and you can add more area to it. Of course, we just told you it was the Shift key, but what if you couldn't remember which key it was? Just press a modifier key (such as Shift, Option/Alt, Command/Control, etc.) then look at your cursor. When you hold the Shift key, a little plus sign appears at the bottom right-hand corner of the cursor to tell you that you can add to the selection. Hold Option (PC: Alt) and a minus sign appears to tell you that you can subtract from the selection. Hold Command (PC: Control) and a pair of scissors appears, telling you that if you click-and-drag the selection, it will cut out the image inside of the selection and move it right along with the cursor.

HOW TO TAME THE SELECT SIMILAR COMMAND

A popular trick for making selections of large areas (such as backgrounds) is to select part of the background that contains most of the colors that appear within that background. Then you can go under the Select menu and choose Similar. Photoshop will then select all the similar colors in your image. This can really speed up the task of selecting an entire background, especially if the background is limited to just a few colors. Here's the tip: Do you know what determines how many pixels out the Similar command selects? Believe it or not, it's controlled by the Magic Wand's Tolerance setting. The higher the setting, the more pixels it selects. Eerie, ain't it? Soooooooo… if you use Similar, and it doesn't select enough colors, go to the Magic Wand tool, increase the Tolerance setting, and then try running Similar again. This all makes perfect sense (at least to an engineer at Adobe).

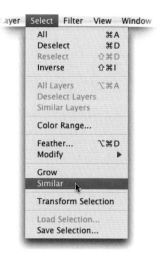

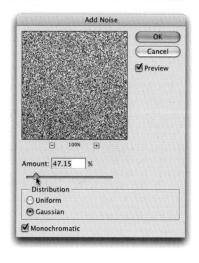

QUICK TRICK TO REAPPLY THAT FILTER

Want a convenient shortcut that lets you run the last filter you applied, without going to the Filter menu? Too bad (just kidding). Simply press Command-F (PC: Control-F). What if you don't want the same settings (ah, I knew you were going to ask that)? Try pressing Command-Option-F (PC: Control-Alt-F), which brings up the dialog for the last filter you applied with the last settings you used.

SCRUBBY SLIDER SHIFT-CLICK TRICK

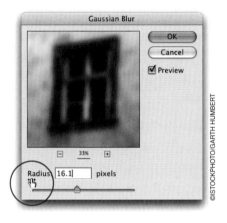

Adobe borrowed scrubby sliders, a very cool feature from Adobe After Effects, and put it in Photoshop. You use it by clicking on a field's name, rather than in the field itself, and the value in the field changes as you drag (scrub) over the field's name. However, it scrubs in very small increments. That is, unless you hold the Shift key, which is ideal when you need to make big changes in the field (like from 0 to 256).

ESCAPE FROM THE CROP TOOL (OR DIE!)

Sometimes when you're using the Crop tool (C), you change your mind and decide not to crop. If this happens to you, do you have to crop and then press the undo shortcut? Nah, press the Escape key to cancel your crop and remove the cropping border. You can also click on the circle with a slash icon (the international symbol for "NO") on the far right of the Options Bar to cancel a crop.

Okay, there's one more way: just switch tools—a dialog will appear asking you if you want to complete the crop or not. Just hit Don't Crop.

⬤ ⬤ ⬤ GETTING THE STARTUP WINDOW BACK

When you first launch Photoshop CS2, it brings up a Welcome Screen that has links to tutorials, a list of what's new, etc. There's also a checkbox at the bottom called Show This Dialog at Startup that you'll probably uncheck before too long, because after a short while the Welcome Screen tends to get on your nerves (that's why Adobe put that checkbox there in the first

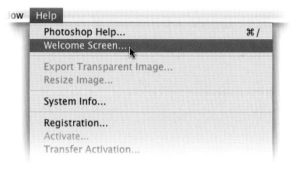

place). However, if you've turned off that checkbox, and then one day you have some extra time and you'd like to explore what the Welcome Screen has to offer, you can temporarily bring it back by going under the Help menu and choosing Welcome Screen.

⬤ ⬤ ⬤ GETTING YOUR WARNINGS BACK (RESETTING ALL DIALOGS)

One thing I love about Photoshop is that a number of warning dialogs have a magical checkbox that says "Don't show this dialog again" (or something along those lines). However, if you later decide you want these warning dialogs put back into play (this is especially helpful if you're training someone new on your computer), you can have them become active again. Just go under the Photoshop menu (PC: Edit menu), under Preferences, and choose General. In the General section of the Preferences dialog, click on the button at the bottom of the dialog named Reset All Warning Dialogs.

THE SMALLER TOOLBOX TRICK

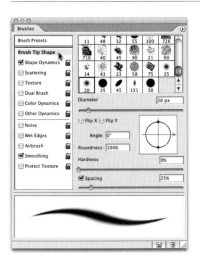

Is that Toolbox taking up too much space, but you don't want to close it, because a few seconds later, sure enough, you'll need a tool? Then just double-click on the very top of your Toolbox and it will tuck up out of the way, leaving just that little tab showing. Need it back fast, just double-click the little tab again and it comes right back.

BRUSHES PALETTE: THAT'S NOT A HEADER, IT'S A BUTTON

If you look in the expanded Brushes palette (docked in the Palette Well by default), there's a list of controls on the left side of the dialog. At the top it shows Brush Presets, and you might figure that you can click on that and get some options, but the one that catches just about everyone off guard is just below that. It's the header for Brush Tip Shape. It appears to be a header for a list of brush tip options below it, but in reality, it's a button (I know, it doesn't look like a button, but it is). Click right on the words "Brush Tip Shape" and the Brush Tip Shape options are revealed in the main panel on the right.

⬤ ⬤ ⬤ DANGEROUS INTERSECTION?

You've already learned that if you're using a selection tool (Lasso, Rectangular Marquee, etc.) and you need to add an additional area to your currently selected area, you can hold the Shift key, then any selection you draw with one of those tools will be added. But what if you have a selection and instead you want to create a new selection that will intersect with your existing selection to create an entirely new selection (Whew! That sounds complicated just explaining it)? Here's how: Draw your first selection, then up in the Options Bar you'll find four icons for various selection options. The fourth icon is Intersect with Selection. Click on it, then draw another selection that overlaps your existing selection and all will become clear (grasshopper).

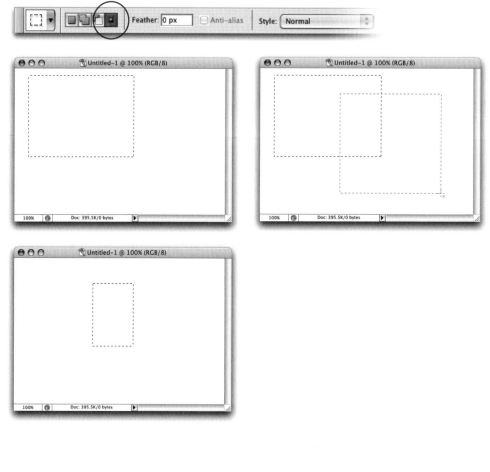

NUDGING 10 PIXELS AT A TIME

As you know, as long as you have the Move tool (V) selected, you can move (or nudge) your current layer using the Up/Down/Left/Right Arrow keys on your keyboard. For every press of an Arrow, it nudges your layer 1 pixel in that direction. However, if you hold the Shift key and use the Arrow keys, it nudges the object 10 pixels at a time.

©ISTOCKPHOTO/BRYCE KROLL

MAKE THAT OPTIONS BAR FLOAT— FLOAT???

You may not realize it, but the Options Bar, which seems permanently docked to the top of your work area, can actually be redocked to the bottom of your screen, or you can make it into a floating palette. To make it float, just click on the little tab on the far-left side of the bar, drag it away, and voilà, it floats. To dock it at the bottom of your screen, drag the tab down to the bottom left-hand side of your screen and it snaps into place. You can even hide the Options Bar altogether by choosing Options from the Window menu. You can always get it back by double-clicking on any tool.

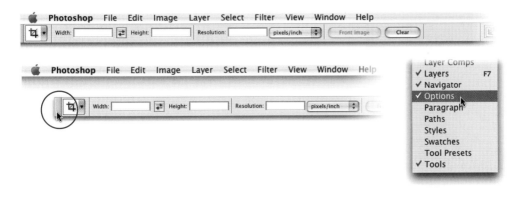

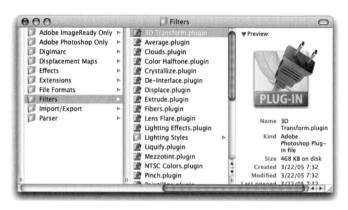

⬤ ⬤ ⬤ WHERE'S THE 3D TRANSFORM FILTER?

You can kill a lot of otherwise productive time searching for the 3D Transform filter that's been in Photoshop for years. That's because—it ain't there. It no longer installs when you install Photoshop, but Adobe thought that somebody, somewhere, might want to use it for something, so even though it doesn't install, you can find it in the Goodies folder on the Photoshop CS2 Resources and Extras disc. Just drag it into Photoshop's Filters folder (inside the Plug-Ins folder) to get it back in your Filter menu (under Render).

⬤ ⬤ ⬤ SUPERSIZE IT

This is a super speed trick for getting your image view up (or down) to size. To instantly view your image at 100% size, double-click on the Zoom tool in the Toolbox. To have your image fit as large as possible on your screen (using the Fit On Screen command), double-click the Hand tool.

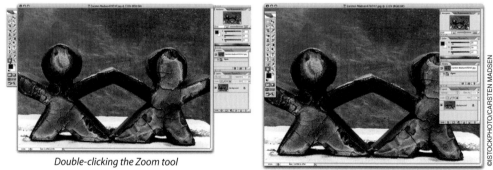

Double-clicking the Zoom tool

Double-clicking the Hand tool

©ISTOCKPHOTO/CARSTEN MADSEN

⬤ ⬤ ⬤ STEAL COLOR FROM ANYWHERE

In previous versions of Photoshop, you could click the Eyedropper tool (I) on any color within your image, and it would steal that color and make it your new Foreground color. The only drawback was you could only steal colors from within an open document window. Back in Photoshop 7.0, Adobe cut the Eyedropper tool loose from the chains that bound it, and now, as long as you click within an open image first, you can drag right out of your image window and sample a color from, well, anywhere. That includes sampling colors from other applications, Photoshop's own Toolbox and menu bars, and even your computer's desktop pattern. Just remember to click in your image first, and then drag that Eyedropper to a new world of color delights that dare not speak its name.

©ISTOCKPHOTO/CARSTEN MADSEN

ASK PHOTOSHOP TO REMEMBER MORE

Photoshop CS2 remembers the last 30 documents that you had open, but by default it only displays the last 10 under the File menu, under Open Recent. However, you're not limited to just 10. Would you rather Photoshop displayed the last 15 instead? Then in Mac OS X, go under the Photoshop menu, under Preferences, and choose File Handling (in Windows, Preferences can be found under the Edit menu). When the dialog appears, under Recent File List Contains, enter the desired number of files (up to 30) that you want to have quick access to under the Open Recent menu.

SHRINK THOSE PALETTES DOWN TO SIZE

Are your palettes in the way, but you don't want to hide them all using the Tab key? You can double-click the palette's name tab, and the palette (and any nested palettes) will minimize to just the tab itself, giving you lots of screen real estate. Need the palette back, just double-click on its tab again.

CREATING THE ÜBER PALETTE

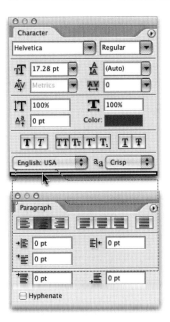

You've been able to nest one or more palettes into another palette since Photoshop 3.0. No big deal, but now you can not only nest but also dock palettes one atop the other, creating a giant über palette. Here's how: Drag the name tab of one palette to the bottom edge of a second palette and slowly drag upward. A thin, black double-line will appear at the bottom of the top palette, letting you know it's "time to dock." Release the mouse button and your palettes will be docked, one on top of the other. Now, when you move the top palette, all docked palettes will move with it as a group.

FIX THOSE TOOL SETTINGS FAST

There's no doubt you'll be "messing" with many, if not all, of the options for the tools you use every day in Photoshop. One day you'll go to use a tool, and you'll have messed with it to the extent that something's just not right. To quickly get back to any tool's default settings, choose the tool from the Toolbox, then Control-click (PC: Right-click) on the tool's icon that appears in the Options Bar on the far left. A contextual menu will appear where you can choose Reset Tool to set it back to its factory-fresh defaults. By the way, while you're there, you can also choose Reset All Tools and they will all revert to their defaults.

BRING ORDER BACK TO YOUR WORLD

In Photoshop, you're constantly moving your palettes around, and before long, you've got one messy set of palettes littering your screen. If your palettes get messy, you're only one simple menu command from having them back at their factory-fresh default locations. Just go under the Window menu, under Workspace, and choose Reset Palette Locations, and all will be right with your world once more (that is, until you mess 'em up again).

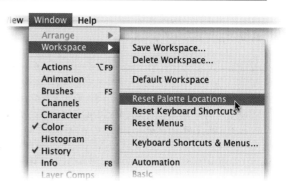

THE UNDOCUMENTED FILL SHORTCUT

There are all sorts of keyboard shortcuts for filling selections, entire layers, and stuff like that, but if you look under the Edit menu, next to the Fill command there's a new little shortcut in CS2 for bringing up the Fill dialog itself (about time!). It's Shift-F5. However, there's an undocumented keyboard shortcut that will do the same trick—it's

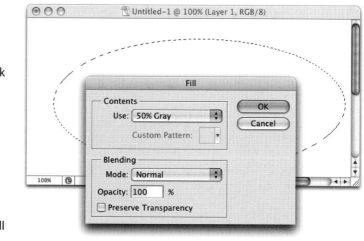

Shift-Delete (PC: Shift-Backspace). This is a good one to pull on your Photoshop buddies and co-workers as a Photoshop trivia question, because few people know it exists.

DESELECTED AND FORGOT TO SAVE? DON'T SWEAT IT

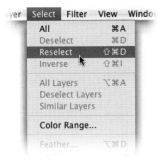

If, after you've created a selection in an image, deselected it, and moved on to other things, you suddenly wish you had that selection back, you're not out of luck. As long as you haven't made another selection (since the one you want to get back), Photoshop remembers your last selection and lets you get it back by going under the Select menu and choosing Reselect. When you choose it, the last selection you created reappears within your image. If you create a selection that, while it's still active, you know you want to keep for later use, then go under the Select menu and choose Save Selection. When the Save Selection dialog appears, click OK, and Photoshop saves it. You can reload it anytime by going under the Select menu and choosing Load Selection. Your selection will be named "Alpha 1" by default, and you can choose to load it (or other subsequent saved selections) from the Channel pop-up menu in the Load Selection dialog.

SUPER-FAST INCHES TO PIXELS

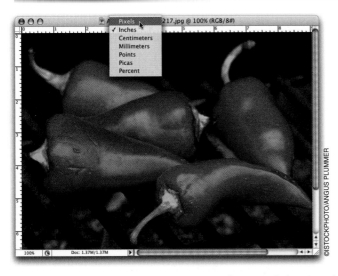

Want to change the unit of measurement for your image? Don't go digging through Photoshop's menus for the Preferences dialog, just Control-click (PC: Right-click) on Photoshop's rulers and a contextual menu will appear with a list of measurement units. (*Note:* If your rulers are not showing, press Command-R [PC: Control-R]). Choose the one you want, and your rulers will instantly reflect the change. If you feel you must access the Units & Rulers Preferences dialog, just double-click anywhere on one of Photoshop's rulers and the dialog will appear.

BOSS AROUND YOUR COLOR SWATCHES

Here are a few tips for using the Swatches palette (found under the Window menu). I'm sure you know that if you click on a color in the Swatches palette, that color becomes your new Foreground color. Here's one you may not have realized—if you Command-click (PC: Control-click) on a swatch, that color now becomes your Background color. Also, you can delete any swatch by holding the Option key (PC: Alt key) and clicking on the swatch you want to remove. You can also add a color to your swatches by setting your Foreground color to the color you want to save and clicking on any open space at the bottom of the Swatches palette.

ZOOMED IN? DON'T USE THE SCROLL BARS

If you've zoomed in on an image, using the scroll bars can be incredibly frustrating, because you move just a tiny bit. Here's how to get around that—don't use the scroll bars. (Okay, there's more to it than that.) Instead, when you're zoomed in, use the Hand tool, but to save time, access it by simply pressing the Spacebar. It temporarily switches you to the Hand, letting you easily navigate through your zoomed image.

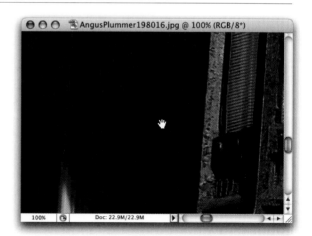

LET PHOTOSHOP DO THE MATH WHEN COPYING/PASTING

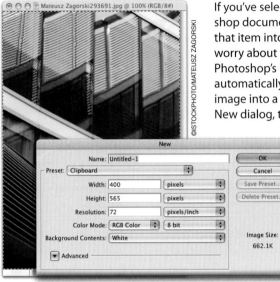

If you've selected something within your Photoshop document and you want to copy-and-paste that item into its own separate document, don't worry about typing the Width and Height into Photoshop's New document dialog. Photoshop automatically figures that you're going to paste that image into a new document, so when you open the New dialog, the exact size of your copied selection has already been entered for you, so just click OK, and then paste your image inside—it'll be a perfect fit.

INSTANT SELECTION FROM ANY PATH

When you're using the Pen tool (P) to create a path, you can go to the Paths palette (under the Window menu) and click on the third icon from the left (at the bottom of the palette) to turn your path into a selection, or you can use the keyboard shortcut Command-Return (PC: Control-Enter). We prefer the keyboard shortcut, because it will do the exact same job faster and saves us from opening the Paths palette, taking up valuable screen real estate. *Note:* If you want to create a selection from an existing path, select that path in the Paths palette and then use the shortcut.

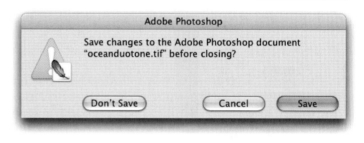

● ● ● SAVE CLICKS WHEN YOU CLOSE

This is such a quick little tip that you might not think that it matters, but it saves a few seconds every time you close a document. If you close a number of documents a day (and my guess is, you do), it really starts to add up fast. When you close a document, Photoshop presents you with a dialog asking, "Save changes to the Adobe Photoshop document before closing?" You have three choices: (1) Don't Save, (2) Cancel, and (3) Save. Here's the shortcut: Press the letter D for Don't Save, press S for Save, and C for Cancel.

● ● ● BEEN BINGEING ON RAM? MAYBE IT'S TIME TO PURGE!

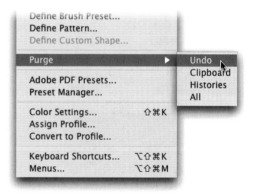

What do you do if the dreaded "Not enough RAM to complete this function" dialog appears? Outside of buying more RAM and installing it on the spot, you might want to purge some of the "junk" hanging around in RAM so you can free up some space to complete the project you're working on. You do this by going under the Edit menu, under Purge, and choosing to empty your Undo, Photoshop's Clipboard, your History States, or everything at once (All). They're in the order you should proceed, so first try purging your Undo and see if that frees up enough memory. If that doesn't do it, try the Clipboard, then Histories. If that doesn't do it, try this super-slick insider tip: Make a tiny (1x1") selection within your document, and then go under the Edit menu and choose Copy three times in a row. Believe it or not, it often works, and has gotten us out of more than one sticky situation.

REACHING THE FREE TRANSFORM HANDLES

If you want to use Free Transform on a layer, but your image extends beyond the edges of your document window (and this happens frequently if you're collaging different photos together), you won't be able to reach the Free Transform handles to scale your image down to size. Here's the keyboard shortcut that lets you reach each and every handle, no matter how far the image extends outside your current canvas area. Just press Command-T (PC: Control-T) to bring up Free Transform, then press Command-0 (zero) (PC: Control-0) and your window will zoom out to exactly the right size to enable you to reach all the handles. Cool!

TRANSFORMING AND COPYING AT THE SAME TIME

Generally, when you apply a transformation to an object (scaling, rotating, distorting, perspective), you apply that transformation to the object itself. However, here's a cool tip if you want to apply a transformation (using Free Transform) on a duplicate of your object, rather than on the original: Press Command-Option-T (PC: Control-Alt-T), then use Free Transform as you usually would. You'll notice that as you begin to transform, the original object remains untouched, and a copy is transformed instead.

Imagine a pig. Wait, not the sloppy grunting kind. Imagine that cute pig from the movie Babe. *Clean, well kempt, with a broad vocabulary and a slightly British accent. Ahh,*

Life in the Fast Lane
production tips

that's better. Now, imagine that he somehow stumbled into a giant vat of grease, jumped out, and began to run at full speed. If you decided to try to catch him with your bare hands (and it's a reasonable assumption that you would), how easy would that be? Now, think of this chapter as "the making of the pig." Now you're the pig, and your competition is trying to catch you. But after learning the tips in this chapter, you're "faster than a greased pig" in Photoshop. Okay, I admit this whole pig thing isn't the greatest metaphor. Let's try this. You're an eagle, a soaring proud bird. And you've somehow fallen into a giant vat of grease. Suddenly, a shot rings out…. I'm not sure I like where this is going. Let's try this: Every day you spend time in Photoshop. Some of it is fun, creative time. Some of it is boring production time, such as making selections, loading brush sets, applying Curves, cropping, transforming—you know, boring stuff. But if you could greatly speed up the boring stuff, that would leave more time for the fun, creative stuff, right? When you strip away all the greased-pig metaphors, that's what this chapter is really about. Run, Babe, run!

MISS THE OLD DEFAULT ACTIONS?

If you miss the old default set of actions that has been shipping with Photoshop for years, you can get it back fairly easily. Just go to the Actions palette's flyout menu and choose Sample Actions to reload that old default set.

REARRANGING YOUR BRUSHES

One of the things in Photoshop that just didn't make sense to us was that you couldn't easily rearrange the order of your brushes in the Brushes palette or Brush Picker. Oh sure, you could create a whole new custom set with the brushes you wanted, in the order you wanted them, but it would take a while, and frankly, was such a pain that we only know a handful of people who actually went through the trouble. Well, our wish for easily rearranging brushes is finally here, but the process is a bit hidden beneath the surface. To move a brush from one spot in the palette to another, go under the Edit menu, and choose Preset Manager. In the Preset Manager dialog, under Preset Type, choose Brushes. Then, click-and-drag the brush of your choice to the location of your choice. At last, we are free to move brushes among the herd.

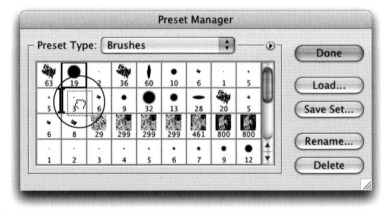

⦿ ⦿ ⦿ FIND THE CENTER OF ANY DOCUMENT

Need to find the exact center of your image? All you need is a layer filled with your Fore-ground color, and Photoshop will do the rest (okay, you have to do a little, but Photoshop will certainly help). First, click on the Create a New Layer icon in the Layers palette and press Option-Delete (PC: Alt-Backspace) to fill it with your Foreground color. Make your rulers visible (press Command-R [PC: Control-R]) and drag a guide down from the top ruler. When you get close to the center of the image, the guide will automatically snap to the exact horizontal center. Do the same with the side ruler, and it automatically snaps to the vertical center of your image. (*Note:* If there's not any snapping going on, be sure Snap is turned on under the View menu.)

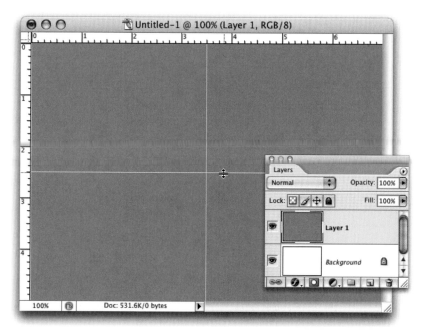

⬤ ⬤ ⬤ NO MORE JAGGY LASSO TOOL SELECTIONS

Have you ever tried to create a smooth selection using the Lasso tool? It's just about impossible, right? (If it sounds like it isn't, give it a try—open a new document, take the Lasso tool, and draw any random selection, and then look at the selection. It's jaggy—not crazy jaggy, but it's certainly not smooth.) If you were trying to create a selection for an interface design, or a realistic element of some sort, it would just be too jaggy to use. Here's a tip:

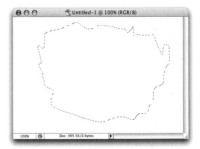

(1) Press L to get the Lasso tool and draw around the area you want to use as your selection.

(2) Press the letter Q to enter Quick Mask mode (your selection will now be surrounded with a reddish hue).

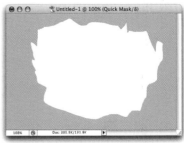

(3) Go under the Filter menu, under Noise, and choose Median. As you move the Radius slider to the right, you'll see your edges smooth out.

(4) When it looks nice and smooth, click OK then press the letter Q again to return to Standard mode, and you'll have nothing but a nice rounded selection.

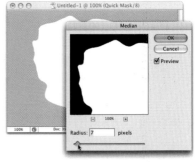

Look at the selection in the first image above. See how those jaggies have been replaced by the smooth edges—courtesy of the Median filter?

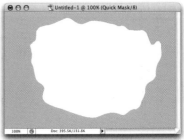

50 **CHAPTER 3 •** Production Tips

OPEN UP SOME SCREEN REAL ESTATE

A lot of times when you're working on a project, your screen can get really cluttered with palettes (Photoshop is an especially palette-heavy application). If you want all the palettes out of the way for your convenience while you're working, just press Shift-Tab to hide them, or Shift-Tab to bring them back. The menu bar, the Options Bar, and the Toolbox will still be visible.

LET PHOTOSHOP DO THE WORK IN CURVES

Let's say you're using the Curves dialog for correcting images and you have an image where you're trying to adjust the color of some green plants. How do you know where that particular green "lives" on the curve so you can dial in and adjust it? Photoshop can tell you—In fact, you can have Photoshop automatically plot that color on the curve for you. With the Curves dialog open, just Command-click (PC: Control-click) on that color within your image. Photoshop will then add a point to the curve that represents the spot you sampled, and now you're ready to tweak it.

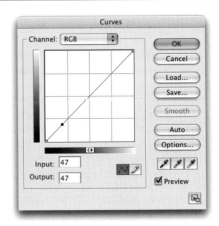

WANT A FINER GRID? YOU GOT IT!

While we're talking Curves, by default the Curves dialog displays a 25% grid. If you'd like a finer grid, you can Option-click (PC: Alt-click) once within the grid, and it will then display a 10% grid.

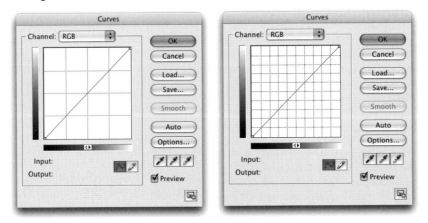

YOU DON'T NEED THE BRUSHES PALETTE TO CHANGE BRUSH SIZE

In Photoshop CS2 you can increase or decrease the size of your brush by 10 pixels by pressing the Left or Right Bracket keys when the Brush tool (B) is selected. Once your brush is more than 100 pixels in size, it then moves in 25-pixel increments; if you go higher than 200 pixels, it moves in 50-pixel increments until you reach 300 pixels, at which point it moves in 100-pixel increments.

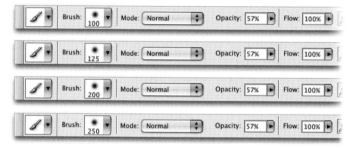

ROTATE TO ANY ANGLE THE FAST WAY

If you have a specific angle that you'd like to rotate a layer to, it's easy. Get the Measure tool (it looks like a ruler and is in the Eyedropper tool's flyout menu in the Toolbox), and click-and-drag out a line at the desired angle. Then go under the Edit menu, under Transform, and choose Rotate. Your layer will instantly rotate to match the angle that you drew with the Measure tool. *Note:* To rotate the Background layer, you must first select it (Command-A [PC: Control-A]).

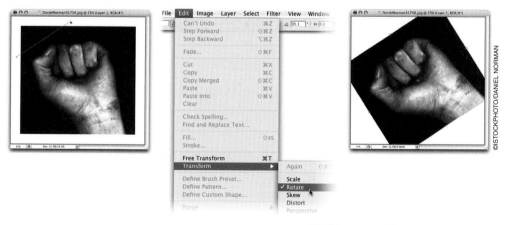

©ISTOCKPHOTO/DANIEL NORMAN

GET RID OF UNWANTED BRUSHES

You probably already know that you can add a brush to the Brushes palette, but did you know that it's even easier to delete them? Just hold the Option key (PC: Alt key) and you'll notice that your cursor changes into a pair of scissors. Click once on the brush you want to delete and that baby's gone—no warning dialog, no chance to change your mind—it's gone.

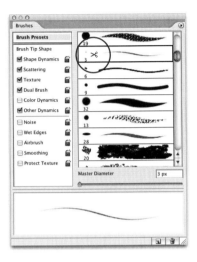

BRUSHES RIGHT WHERE YOU WANT 'EM

Here's a tip that gives you a faster and more convenient way to switch to another preset brush without using the Brushes palette—and you might find that you like it even better. Just press the Control key, then click within your image (PC: Right-click) and the Brush Picker will appear directly under your cursor. Plus, you can even change the Master Diameter of the brush that you choose in the Picker. This is one you'll have to try to appreciate the sheer speed and convenience of putting your brushes at your fingertips anytime.

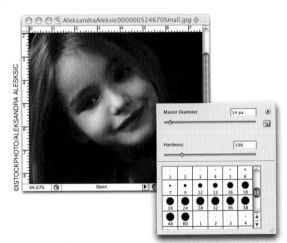

NAVIGATING THE BRUSH PICKER LIKE A PRO

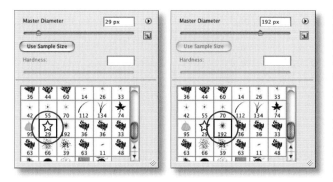

Now that you've learned how to bring up the Brush Picker right where you want it, it wouldn't hurt to learn this quick navigation tip to keep you from spending more time there than necessary. Once you've selected a brush in the Picker, just use the Arrow keys on your keyboard to navigate up, down, left, or right to other brushes in the Picker. Once you choose a brush and you are no longer in the Brush Picker, you can use the Period and Comma keys to move forward and backward through the different brushes. Shift-Comma and Shift-Period will jump you to the first and last brushes in the Brush Picker, respectively.

GET MORE CONTROL OVER YOUR PAINT STROKES

Photoshop lets you affect a brush stroke even after you've painted it by using Photoshop's Fade command (found under the Edit menu). Fade works like "undo on a slider," and dragging the Opacity slider all the way to the left will completely undo your freshly painted brush stroke, but if you stop anywhere before the far-left side, it will instead simply lighten the stroke. You can also use the Mode pop-up menu to alter how your stroke blends with the object below it.

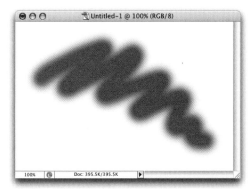

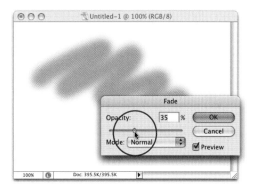

SPEED TIP TO ROTATE THROUGH OPEN IMAGES

Have a bunch of images open on your
screen and can't see the one you want?
Just press Control-Tab to move from one
open image to the next, cycling through
all of your open documents.

INSTANTLY FIND THE CENTER OF ANY OBJECT

This is a great tip for quickly finding the exact
center of any object on its own layer. You start by
pressing Command-T (PC: Control-T) to bring up
the Free Transform bounding box. The bounding
box has a handle in the center of both sides and
center handles at both the top and bottom. Now
all you have to do is make Photoshop's rulers
visible (Command-R [PC: Control-R]), and then
drag out a horizontal and a vertical ruler guide
to these handles to mark the center. Better still, if
you have the Snap command active in the View
menu, the guides will snap to the center of your
object as you drag.

 **MAKING YOUR GUIDE FLIP**

Just like most page-layout applications, Photoshop has non-printing guides you can pull out anytime you need to align objects or type, but there's also a trick for flipping the guides. To access the guides, make your rulers visible by pressing Command-R (PC: Control-R), then click-and-hold within one of the rulers and drag out a guide. If you pull out a horizontal guide from the top ruler, but really wanted a vertical guide, just press the Option key (PC: Alt key) as you drag and your guide will flip from horizontal to vertical (pretty slick). You can pull out as many guides as you need (there's probably a limit to how many you can use, but we've never reached it). When you're done using a guide, just use the Move tool (V) to drag it back to the ruler where it came from. To remove all of your guides at once, choose Clear Guides from the View menu.

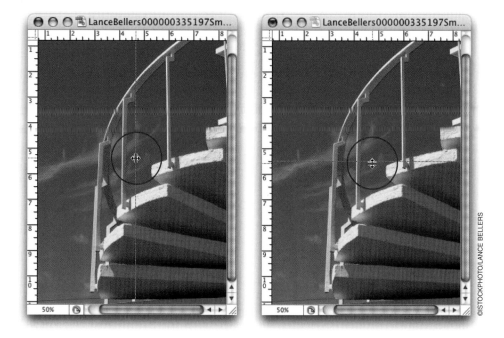

©ISTOCKPHOTO/LANCE BELLERS

CREATING TEMPORARY BRUSHES

It's easy to create a temporary brush based on your preset brushes in Photoshop. Just click on the Brush thumbnail in the Options Bar to bring up the Brush Picker. Using the Master Diameter slider, you can change your brush size from 1 to 2500 pixels. If you like the size of your new brush and you want to save it, just click the Create a New Brush Preset icon at the top right of the dialog. The Brush Name dialog will appear so you can name your new brush. When you click OK, the new brush will immediately be added to your Brush Picker (and Brushes palette).

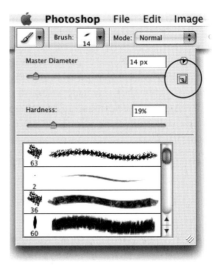

REUSING YOUR LAST CURVE SETTING

Once you've applied a curve setting to an image, it's very possible that you'd like to use that exact same setting again, or maybe you'd just like to tweak that setting a bit. Well, you can. To bring up the Curves dialog with the last curve you used still in place, press Command-Option-M (PC: Control-Alt-M).

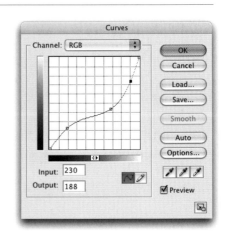

⬤ ⬤ ⬤ BRINGING BACK THOSE CROPPED-AWAY AREAS

When you're using the Crop tool (C) to crop images, you'll find that you actually have some options on how the area you're cropping away is handled after the crop. For example, in the Options Bar (as long as you're not on the Background layer) you'll see an option that lets you either Delete the cropped areas or simply Hide them from view (in other words, the areas are still there, they just expand out into the canvas area). If you choose the Hide option, it crops the image window down to the size of the crop, but since the cropped-away areas are still really there, you can use the Move tool (V) to drag these cropped areas back into view.

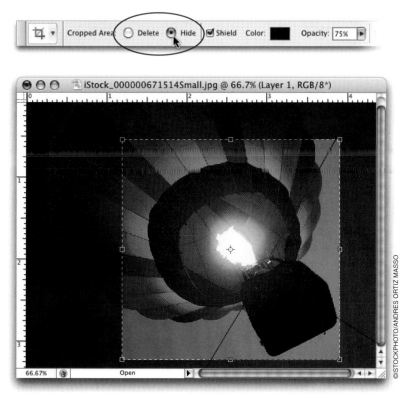

©ISTOCKPHOTO/ANDRES ORTIZ MASSO

FIX THOSE STRAY PIXELS FAST!

Sometimes when making a selection with the Magic Wand tool (W) or Color Range command (under the Select menu), Photoshop will leave little stray pixels unselected. You can tell where they are because they appear to twinkle on and off, kind of teasing…nay, taunting you, because your selection is not complete. Luckily, there's a quick way to rein in those renegade stray pixels. Go under the Select menu, under Modify, and choose Smooth. Enter a Sample Radius of 1 pixel and click OK. That will usually do the trick—those stray pixels are now selected.

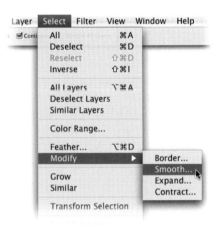

GETTING MORE CONTROL OVER THE MAGIC WAND

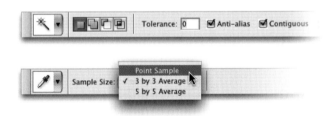

By default, the Eyedropper tool's Sample Size feature (in the Options Bar) is set to Point Sample, which comes into play if you're using it to read values for color correction. But for now, it's important to know that the Sample Size option chosen for the Eyedropper tool (I) actually affects how the Magic Wand tool (W) makes its selection (the two have an undocumented relationship). If you increase the Eyedropper's Sample Size to 3 by 3 or 5 by 5 Average, the Magic Wand will select an average of a much larger range of pixels in the sample area. This is important to know, because if you don't have Point Sample chosen and you set the Magic Wand Tolerance to 0, it won't just select the individual pixel you click on—it will select all of the pixels that match any of the pixels in a 3 by 3 or 5 by 5 area. The next time your Magic Wand isn't behaving the way it used to, check to see if you have changed the Eyedropper tool's Sample Size.

MAKING THE COLOR PALETTE WORK TWICE AS HARD

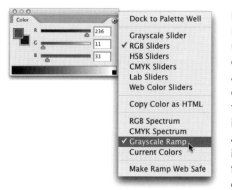

If you use the Color palette (under the Window menu) to select colors, you're probably already using the color ramp at the bottom of the palette for making quick color selections, but here are two tips that make using the ramp faster and easier. First, the color ramp doesn't have to use the same color mode as the color sliders above it; for example, you can have RGB for your sliders and grayscale as your ramp. This is great because it gives you two different models to choose from without digging through menus. You can choose the color modes for both the sliders and the ramp from the Color palette's flyout menu. The second tip is that if you quickly want to change color ramps, Shift-click on the ramp. Every time you Shift-click, it will rotate to the next color mode.

USE YOUR LAST SETTINGS AND SAVE TIME

This is a tip that will save you time when you're making tonal adjustments using Levels, Curves, Color Balance, etc. (most anything that appears under the Adjustments submenu under the Image menu). When you bring up one of the tonal adjustment dialogs, it always displays its default settings, but if you hold the Option key (PC: Alt key) when choosing it from the Adjustments menu, instead of coming up with the default settings, it will display the last settings you used in that particular dialog. You can also add the Option (PC: Alt) key to the keyboard shortcuts. For example, the shortcut to bring up the Levels dialog is Command-L (PC: Control-L), but if you add Option (PC: Alt) to those keys, the Levels dialog will open with your last-used settings.

● ● ● HIT THOSE CHANNELS FAST

When you're in the Curves dialog (Command-M [PC: Control-M]), if you're charging by the hour, you can certainly travel up to the Channel pop-up menu and choose each individual channel you want to work on, but if you want to do it the fast way, just press Command-1 for Red, Command-2 for Green, and Command-3 for Blue (PC: Control-1, Control-2, etc.). If you need to return to the composite RGB channel, press Command-Tilde (PC: Control-Tilde). By the way, the Tilde key looks like ~, and it lives right above the Tab key on your keyboard. Don't feel bad. Nobody knows what the Tilde key is. We're not sure it's a real symbol at all. We think it was made up so there wouldn't be an empty space there on your keyboard. Hey, it's somewhat plausible.

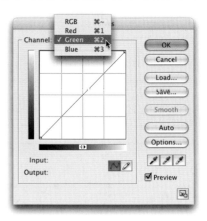

● ● ● HOW TO GET AN UNDO AFTER YOU'VE CLOSED THE DOCUMENT

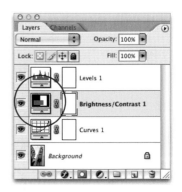

As you probably already know, the History palette keeps track of the last 20 changes to your document, and you can use it for multiple undos when working on a project. The only bad part is that when you close your document, your undos (in History) are automatically deleted. However, there is a way to save an undo, as long as it's a tonal adjustment (such as Curves, Levels, Color Balance, etc.), by creating adjustment layers. Just click on the half-white/half-black circle icon at the bottom of the Layers palette and choose your tonal adjustment from the pop-up menu to create an adjustment layer. These adjustment layers are saved along with your file. That way, the next time you open the file, you can go back and edit your Curves, Levels, etc., adjustment by double-clicking on the adjustment layer's thumbnail. The last-applied adjustment will appear, and you can edit it live. If you decide you don't want the original adjustment applied at all, you can drag the adjustment layer into the Trash icon at the bottom of the Layers palette. You can also add a Gradient fill, a Pattern fill, and even a Solid Color fill as an adjustment layer, giving you an undo at a later date, because again, they're saved as layers with the file.

USING THE PEN? STAY AWAY FROM THE TOOLBOX

Want to save trips to the Toolbox when using the Pen tool (P)? You're in luck. Better yet, you don't even have to hold down any modifier keys (such as Option/Alt, etc.), because

Photoshop will do the work for you. Here's why: When you draw a path, move your cursor over a line segment and your Pen cursor automatically changes to the Add Anchor Point tool, so you can click anywhere along that path to add a point. Move your cursor over an existing point, and it changes into the Delete Anchor Point tool (click on the point, and it's deleted). This is called Auto Add/Delete, and it's on by default (you can turn it off, should you want to, using the checkbox in the Options Bar).

PUT YOUR GRADIENT PICKER AT YOUR FINGERTIPS

Want to make the Gradient Picker appear where your cursor is in your image window? You can do this when you have the Gradient tool (G) active, allowing access to your gradient library, by Control-clicking (PC: Right-clicking) within your image area. It also works with the Custom Shape Picker. Here's an even slicker trick: You can use the Return or Enter key instead to bring up the Gradient or Custom Shape Pickers.

⊖ ⊖ ⊖ DON'T CLICK IN THAT FIELD!

Those tiny little fields up in the Options Bar can really be a pain sometimes, especially if you're trying to highlight a field, delete the current value, and type in a new one. Instead of doing all that, just click on the field's name and Photoshop will automatically highlight the entire field for you. That way, you can just type in new

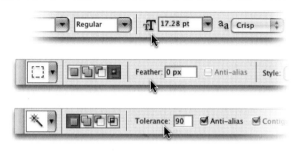

values and it will automatically replace the old values. Great thing is, this doesn't just work in the Options Bar; it works in many of Photoshop's palettes, including the Character and Paragraph palettes.

⊖ ⊖ ⊖ OUT OF MEMORY? TRY THIS FIRST

Here's a tip for avoiding those nasty out-of-memory warning dialogs. One of the reasons Photoshop needs so much memory is that by default it keeps a snapshot of the last 20 things you did to your document, thus allowing you to undo your previous 20 steps. (You can see the running list of your last 20 steps in the History palette.) As you might expect, storing 20 steps takes a mighty chunk of memory, and if you're running a little low (or getting those evil out-of-memory

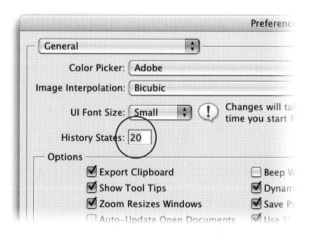

warnings), one thing you might try is lowering the amount of steps Photoshop stores. In Mac OS X, go under the Photoshop menu, under Preferences, under General, and you'll find a field for History States. (In Windows you'll find Preferences under the Edit menu.) You can lower this number (try 8 States for starters), and you may avoid the dreaded memory warnings. Just remember, by lowering the States, you don't have 20 undos anymore.

⬤ ⬤ ⬤ HOW TO "UNERASE"

You probably already know that you can use the History Brush (Y) as an "undo" on a brush, and that by default, the History Brush paints back to how your image looked when you first opened it. But did you know that the Eraser tool has a similar function? That's right; the next time you've got the Eraser tool (E) active, look up in the Options Bar and you'll see a checkbox for Erase to History. Normally, the Eraser tool erases to your Background color, but when you turn on this checkbox, it erases back to what the image looked like when you opened it.

©ISTOCKPHOTO/JOHANNA GOODYEAR

⬤ ⬤ ⬤ LET PHOTOSHOP STRAIGHTEN YOUR CROOKED SCANS

That's right—straightening is totally automated in Photoshop CS2. In fact, try out this ideal situation: Toss two or three photos casually onto your scanner bed, without taking the time to carefully align them, and scan them all with just one pass of your scanner. Then, open the single scan of the three photos in Photoshop, go under the File menu, under Automate, and choose Crop and Straighten Photos. Photoshop will then crop, straighten, and even put each photo into its own separate document. Nice.

COPY ONE LAYER, OR COPY 'EM ALL

If you're working on a layered document, and you make a selection and copy that selection, by default Photoshop only copies the information on your currently active layer (and that's a good thing). However, there may be times when you want to copy your selection as if the image was flattened (in other words, you want to copy everything on all visible layers). If that's the case, press Command-Shift-C (PC: Control-Shift-C), and you'll copy as if the image was flattened, not just on the active layer.

©ISTOCKPHOTO/ANDREAS GUSKOS

STUCK IN A FIELD? HERE'S HOW TO ESCAPE

This is one of those tips that keeps you from pulling your hair out. Sometimes when you're editing values in a field (for example, you're typing numbers in the Opacity field for a layer) and you've entered the number you want, Photoshop doesn't automatically take you out of that field (meaning your cursor is still flashing in the Opacity field). It gets worse if you've switched to another layer (besides the Background layer) and you want to use a

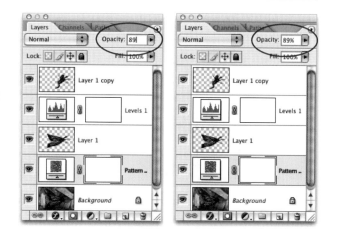

keyboard shortcut to switch tools. For example, you press the letter T to switch to the Type tool, but instead of getting the Type tool, you get an error sound because your cursor is still in the Opacity field (you can't type letters in a number field). Here's how to get around it: Just press the Return (PC: Enter) key on your keyboard to lock in the change in your field and release your keyboard for other tasks.

⬤ ⬤ ⬤ DON'T CANCEL; RESET AND SAVE TIME

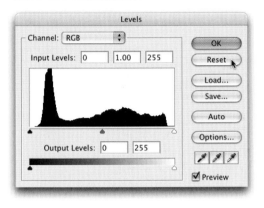

Most of Photoshop's dialogs (but not all) will let you use this little tip, which can save you loads of time. When you're making changes in a dialog (let's use the Levels dialog as an example) and decide that you don't like the changes you've made, one option is to click the Cancel button to close the dialog, leaving your image unchanged. Then you can reopen the dialog and try again. This is an incredible waste of valuable time, so instead, Photoshop lets you "reset" the dialog—putting the settings back to what they were when you first opened it. Just hold the Option key (PC: Alt key) and look at the Cancel button—it changes into the Reset button. Click it, and it resets the dialog automatically, as if you hadn't made any changes at all. Big, big time saver.

⬤ ⬤ ⬤ SEE EVERY TWEAK WITH BIGGER FILTER GALLERY PREVIEWS

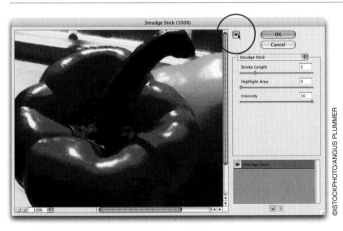

Once you've chosen a filter from the Filter Gallery (under the Filter menu), you'll probably want to spend some time tweaking the settings. If that's the case, you'll also need to see a larger preview of your work so you can really see the effects of each little tweak. You can do that by clicking on the triangle button, to the left of the OK button. This hides the center column (the list of filters) and expands the Preview pane into its space, giving you the full preview experience.

SHOWING ONE EFFECT IN THE FILTER GALLERY

The idea behind the Filter Gallery (under the Filter menu) is the stacking up of one filter on top of the next, but if you want to see any one of the filters by itself, just Option-click (PC: Alt-click) on the Eye icon beside that filter in the filter stack, and all the other filters will be hidden from view. Option-click (PC: Alt-click) on the same Eye icon to bring them all back into view.

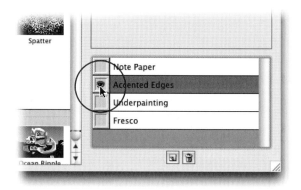

USE THE MOVE TOOL ANYTIME

When you're using just about any of Photoshop's tools, you can temporarily switch to the Move tool at any time by simply holding the Command key (PC: Control key). It's temporary, and as soon as you release it, you're back to the tool you started with.

©ISTOCKPHOTO/ELVIRA OOMENS

FILTER GALLERY ZOOM QUICK TIP

If you're in the Filter Gallery (under the Filter menu) and want to zoom quickly to a particular level of magnification, just Control-click (PC: Right-click) anywhere within the preview window and a contextual menu of zoom views will appear.

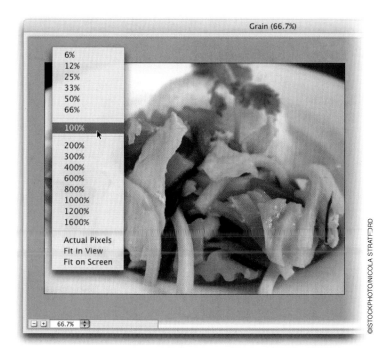

Why is this chapter named "Way Cool Tips"? It's because "Boring Regular Tips" was already taken (psych!). Actually, it's because this is where a lot of the really cool tips wound

Greased Lightnin'
way cool tips

up that didn't fit into any of the other categories. I don't really have anything else to say about this chapter, so instead, let's fill this space by singing a verse of "Greased Lightnin'" from the motion picture Grease. "We'll get some overhead lifters, and four-barrel quads, oh yeah (keep talkin', whoa, keep talkin'). Fuel-injection cutoff and chrome-plated rods, oh yeah (I'll get the money, I'll see you get the money), with the four-speed on the floor, they'll be waitin' at the door, you know that ain't no…." Hey, wait a minute—that next word is a cuss word. Okay, no problem, we'll skip over that word and continue, "…we'll be getting lots of…." Gees, another nasty word. I've been singing that song for years and never really noticed how nasty it was. Just to be safe, let's just jump to the end of the chorus, "…you know that I ain't braggin', she's a real…." Oh, that's just wrong! I'm stopping right here.

FIND THINGS FAST BY COLOR-CODING THEM

If there are particular areas of Photoshop you use a lot, you can make finding them in the menus even faster by color-coding your favorite menu items. Here's how: Go under the Edit menu and choose Menus. When the dialog appears, scroll down to the menu you want and double-click on it. Now scroll down until you find the command you want to color-code, and then click on the word "None" to the far right of that item (under the Color column) and a menu of colors will appear. Choose the color you want for that item, and from now on it will appear highlighted in that color. This is ideal if you're training new Photoshop users. For example, you could color-code certain items for when they're doing prepress (maybe make those items appear in red) and choose another color for when they're designing Web graphics.

USING CAMERA RAW IMAGES AS SMART OBJECTS

You can add any RAW image to your existing document as a Smart Object. Just use the Place command (under the File menu) and navigate your way to the RAW image. When you choose the RAW image, Photoshop will first open Camera Raw so you can process it. When you click Open in the Camera Raw dialog, it will place itself into your document as a Smart Object (and it will have a bounding box around it so you can determine the size you want it to appear within your document). Once you've sized the placed image, press Return (PC: Enter) to lock it into position. If you need to make any edits to the RAW photo after it's placed into your document as a Smart Object, just double-click on the Smart Object's thumbnail in the Layers palette and your RAW image will reopen in Camera Raw. Make your changes, click OK, and it will automatically update in your main document. Sweeeeeettttt!

GETTING MORE CONTROL OVER VANISHING POINT

When you apply the Vanishing Point filter, by default it applies the effect to your Background layer, which means once Vanishing Point "does its thing," you don't have any control over the results. If it's too light, too dark, you want to change the color, blend mode, etc., you're out of luck. That's why, before you run the Vanishing Point filter, you should create a new blank layer by clicking on the Create a New Layer icon at the bottom of the Layers palette. That way, the object (text, whatever) to which you apply Vanishing Point winds up on its own separate layer, where you can control everything from color to opacity and more.

⬤ ⬤ ⬤ TURNING YOUR VANISHING POINT GRID

Need to wrap your Vanishing Point filter grid around a corner? No sweat—just hold the Command key (PC: Control key), drag a center point, and the grid will bend around the corner.

⬤ ⬤ ⬤ HIDDEN ZOOM FEATURE IN VANISHING POINT

If you're using Vanishing Point and need to quickly zoom in on an area, just move your cursor over that area, then press-and-hold the letter X on your keyboard to zoom in on the area where your cursor is. To zoom back out, release the X key.

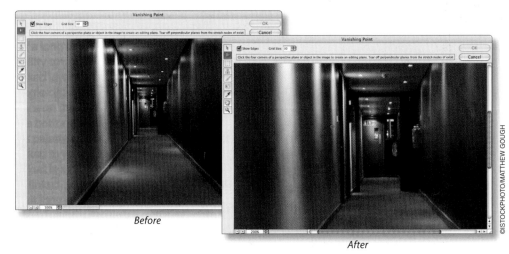

Before

After

THINK YOU MIGHT CHANGE SIZES? MAKE IT A SMART OBJECT!

If you're building a collage, or some other document that has images on different layers, and you think you might wind up resizing some of the images, rather than just dragging-and-dropping opened photos into your main document, make them Smart Objects. That way, when you resize them (especially helpful if you increase their size), it calls upon the original image to make a clean resize (instead of a blurry, pixelated version). To create a Smart Object, you only have to change one thing—instead of opening the photo, go under the File menu and choose Place instead.

MAKING A SMART OBJECT DUMB—WELL, KINDA

If you're using CS2's Smart Objects (by using the Place command under the File menu to add images to your document rather than opening them and dragging-and-dropping them in with the Move tool [V]), you'll also want to know how to convert your Smart Object layer into a regular ol' layer. To do that, click on the Smart Object layer, then go under the Layer menu, under Smart Objects, and choose Convert to Layer.

SWITCHING FROM WARP TO FREE TRANSFORM (AND BACK AGAIN)

If you're using
CS2's Warp Image
feature (which
is accessed by
pressing Command-T [PC: Control-T] to bring up Free Transform, then Control-clicking [PC:
Right-clicking] inside the Free Transform bounding box and choosing Warp from the contextual menu), there's a good chance you'll need to resize the image once you start warping it. If
that happens, there's a button you can click that will switch back to Free Transform. It's near
the top-right corner of the Options Bar, and clicking the button will toggle you between Warp
and Free Transform.

INSTANT THUMBNAIL SIZE CONTROL

Want to change the size of your thumbnail
preview in your Layers, Channels, or Paths
palette? Just hold the Control key (PC: Right-
click) and click in an open area of the palette
(such as the space under your Background
layer, or beneath the bottom channel in the
Channels palette), and a pop-up menu of
thumbnail sizes will appear. For instance, in
the Layers palette you can choose from No,
Small, Medium, or Large Thumbnails, instantly
changing your thumbnail view.

WHAT'S SMARTER THAN USING GUIDES?

Oh wait. I know this one. It's…it's…Smart Guides! (That's right, for 500 points.) These little below-the-radar additions to CS2 are there to help you align objects on layers, but they don't show up just on the edges of your object. As you drag your layer, they look for angles and corners within your layer, and the guides then extend out from there. That's why they're called "Smart." To turn them on within your multilayered file, all you have to do is go under the View menu, under Show, and choose Smart Guides. Once they're enabled, they appear automatically as you drag. They're handier—and smarter—than you'd think.

⬤ ⬤ ⬤ GETTING BACK TO THE FILTER GALLERY DEFAULTS

Let's say you've tried all the filters in the
Filter Gallery, and changed each setting
so much that you can't remember what
the default, out-of-the-box settings were.
Well, you're out of luck (kidding). Here's
a trick for getting back to those default
settings for any filter the Filter Gallery
supports (like any of the Artistic filters,
the Sketch filters, etc.): Open one of these
filters (by choosing it from the Filter menu)
and when it opens in the Filter Gallery,
press-and-hold the Command key (PC:
Control key) and you'll see that the Cancel button changes into the Default button. Click it
(while still holding down Command/Control) and the default settings will magically reappear.

⬤ ⬤ ⬤ HAVING HISTORY TRACK YOUR LAYER VISIBILITY

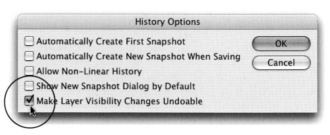

By default, the History palette
tracks the last 20 things you
did in Photoshop, but (weird
as this may sound) it doesn't
track when you hide or show
a layer. For some reason, it
just doesn't record that. Well,
that is unless you know this
tip: Go to the History palette's flyout menu and choose History Options. When the History
Options dialog appears, turn on the checkbox for Make Layer Visibility Changes Undoable.
Now, you can undo your showing and hiding of layers from the History palette.

THE TRICK TO TRICKY EXTRACTIONS

Adobe's own Julieanne Kost (Photoshop guru and instructor supreme) showed this at the Photoshop World Conference & Expo, and it had everybody's jaw dropping, but little has been said of it since, even though it's built into Photoshop CS2's Extract function (found under the Filter menu). It's called Textured Image and you use it when you're dealing with a tough extraction—a person with a dark shirt posing on a dark background, for example—and Extract can't really tell where the shirt ends and the background begins. Turning this on helps detect the edges by examining the texture, and if it detects a texture (like you might find in a shirt), it can often help pull you out of a tight situation.

ZOOMING ALL YOUR TILED IMAGES AT ONCE

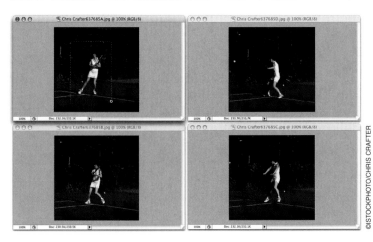

©ISTOCKPHOTO/CHRIS CRAFTER

If you've chosen to tile your open windows (in the Window menu, under Arrange, choose Tile Horizontally [or Vertically]), in Photoshop CS2 you get some hidden functionality. If you want all the tiled images to be displayed at the same level of magnification, just hold the Shift key, grab the Zoom tool (Z), zoom in on one of the images, and all the other tiled images will jump to that same magnification. This is great when you're trying to compare a number of similar images for detail.

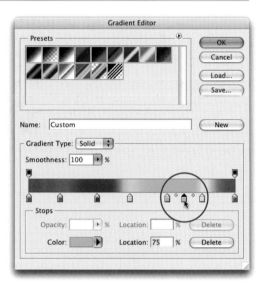

HOW TO DUPLICATE A COLOR STOP

Here's the scenario: You're making a custom gradient using the Gradient tool (G) (by double-clicking the gradient thumbnail in the Options Bar to get to the Gradient Editor) and you need to duplicate one or more of the color stops. No problem. Once you've created one gradient color stop, you can make copies by Option-dragging (PC: Alt-dragging) it. Also, as long as you keep the Option key (PC: Alt key) down while you drag, you can jump right over other existing stops. It's a color stop love fest, can you feel it?

REMOVING EDGE FRINGE WHEN COLLAGING

Any time you're creating a collage, you'll eventually add an image that has little white pixels around the edges of your object. Here's a tip for getting rid of that "fringe." Go under the Layer menu, under Matting, and choose Defringe. Try the default setting of 1 pixel and click OK. What this does (here's the techno speak) is replace the edge pixels with a combination of the pixel colors in

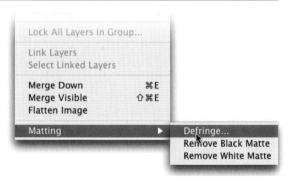

your object and the colors in the background (whew, that hurt). That usually does the trick. If it doesn't, undo it, then try a 2- or 3-pixel Defringe.

CRACKING THE EASTER EGG MYSTERY

Merlin Lives!

Begone

Easter Eggs are usually funny little messages hidden within an application (engineer humor just cracks us up). Photoshop has a few of its own, but one of the lesser-known Easter Eggs is Merlin Lives. To see this Easter Egg, go to the Paths palette (under the Window menu), hold the Option key (PC: Alt key), and in the palette's flyout menu, choose Palette Options. When you do, a tiny floating palette will appear with a picture of Merlin and just one button named "Begone," which closes the dialog. I have to party with those engineer guys.

UNDO ON A SLIDER!

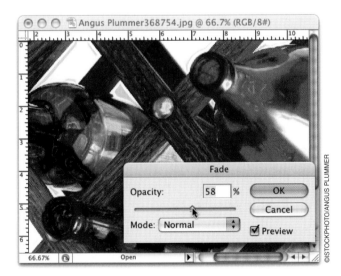

©ISTOCKPHOTO/ANGUS PLUMMER

If you apply a technique (such as a filter or a paint stroke) and the effect is too intense, you can always undo the effect by pressing Command-Z (PC: Control-Z). But if you just want to decrease the intensity, instead of completely undoing it, go under the Edit menu and choose Fade. Want a less intense effect? Just move the Opacity slider to the left. The farther you drag, the less intense the effect. Drag all the way to the left, and the effect is undone.

RESIZING PATHS THE EASY WAY

When you're working with paths, you can visually resize your path by using the Path Selection tool. To do this, press A to get the tool, then go up in the Options Bar and turn on the checkbox for Show Bounding Box. This puts a Free Transform-like bounding box around your path, and you can use this bounding box to resize your path by dragging the handles (remember to hold the Shift key to resize it proportionately).

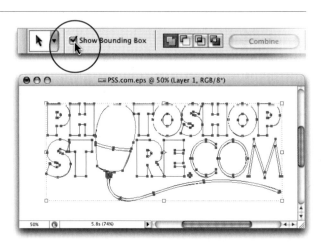

THE GAUSSIAN BLUR KEYBOARD SHORTCUT

I thought that would get your attention. That's because you know there's no keyboard shortcut for applying a Gaussian Blur. But there is in my copy of Photoshop CS2. How is that possible? Because I created one, and you can too. Just go under the Edit menu and choose Keyboard Shortcuts to bring up the Keyboard Shortcuts dialog. Then, from the Shortcuts For pop-up menu, choose Application Menus. In the list of menus in the window beneath it, double-click on Filter to reveal all the choices under the Filter menu. Scroll down to Gaussian Blur, then click on its name. This brings up a field where you can enter the shortcut by pressing the keys you want to use. I recommend using Option-Shift-Command-G (PC: Alt-Shift-Control-G) because there are so few shortcuts not already being used by Photoshop. Click OK, and not only is the shortcut activated but your custom shortcut now appears in the Filter menu to the right of Gaussian Blur.

THE ADVANTAGE OF PHOTO FILTER ADJUSTMENT LAYERS

One of the most brilliant things Adobe did when they added Photo Filters to Photoshop (these filters replicate the old traditional screw-on lens filters) was to make them adjustment layers. You can create one by clicking on the Create New Adjustment Layer pop-up menu in the Layers palette and choosing Photo Filter. After you apply a Photo Filter from the resulting dialog (let's say, for example, you used Warming Filter 81 to warm a cool photo), you can get the Brush tool (B), set your Foreground color to black, and paint over any areas of the photo you don't want to be warmed. This gives you a level of flexibility you wouldn't get any other way.

MAKE A PHOTOSHOP CLIENT PRESENTATION

To hide all your palettes and all your menus, and to display your current image centered on your monitor with a cool black frame around your image, just press the letter F twice, then press the Tab key (F, F, Tab). To return to your regular Photoshop work area, press F, then Tab. You'll be the envy of all your friends, and eventually they'll write folk songs about you. It's almost embarrassing.

⦿ ⦿ ⦿ MOVING YOUR IMAGE IN FULL SCREEN MODE

In Photoshop CS2 you can pull off something users have been wanting for years—the ability to change the placement of your entire image once you're in Full Screen mode (where your image is centered onscreen, surrounded by a black border with no menus, palettes, or tools visible). Just enter Full Screen mode (press F, F, then Tab), hold the Space-bar, and your cursor

will change into the Hand tool. Click-and-drag your entire image anywhere on the screen you'd like. To return to regular mode, press F, then Tab.

⦿ ⦿ ⦿ PHOTO-RETOUCHING SAFETY TIP

Here's a tip that many photo retouchers use—do all your retouching on a layer above your image. That way, you don't damage the underlying image, and you have control over opacity and blend modes you normally wouldn't have. It's also easy to erase areas you wish you hadn't retouched. The key to making this work is to get the Clone Stamp tool (S) and in the Options Bar, turn on the Sample All Layers option. That way you can sample from the underlying image and then paint on the layer above it (believe it or not, by default Photoshop doesn't let you do that—it only lets you clone from the active layer to that same layer).

⦿ ⦿ ⦿ LIGHTS, CAMERA, ACTION: SLIDE SHOWS USING PHOTOSHOP

©ISTOCKPHOTO

Shift-click to see multiple photos in Full Screen mode.

You can create a mock slide show presentation by opening multiple images in Photoshop and then pressing Control-Tab to rotate through the images. Plus, you can hold the Shift key and click on the Full Screen Mode icon near the bottom of your Toolbox to allow your images to fill the full screen (holding Shift will switch all of your open images to the Full Screen mode at once). Press Tab to hide your palettes and you're all set to give a slick presentation. To exit your mini-slide show, press Tab to see the Toolbox, and then Shift-click on the Standard Mode icon.

Shift-click to exit your slide show in Full Screen mode.

PHOTOSHOP'S HIDDEN STEP AND REPEAT

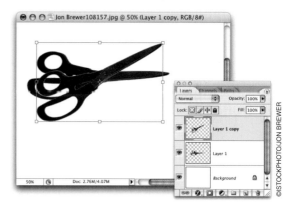

Although Photoshop doesn't have a visible Step and Repeat function (like many vector or page-layout programs do), it still has the feature—it's just a bit hidden. For example, let's say you have an object on a layer, and you want to duplicate and move or rotate that object a number of times in succession (a typical step-and-repeat), here's how you can do it in Photoshop CS2: Start by going to the original layer with the object, then press Command-Option-T (PC: Control-Alt-T) to bring up a special version of Free Transform. Now you can transform your object (move it, rotate it, skew it, etc.), then press Return (PC: Enter) to lock in your transformation. You'll notice that your original object remains untouched on its layer and you now have a new layer with the transformed object. Now press Command-Option-Shift-T (PC: Control-Alt-Shift-T) and this will create a duplicate of your last move, and at the same time it creates a new layer, thereby giving you a step-and-repeat (you have to try this once, and you'll immediately "get it").

PAUSING FOR A BRUSH PREVIEW

If you're choosing your brush tips from the expanded Brushes palette, you don't have to actually click on a brush to see the large preview of it at the bottom of the Brushes palette (which is nested in the Palette Well by default). Instead, pause your cursor right over the brush you want to preview, and in just a second the preview will appear, even though you didn't actually click on the brush tip. The catch is: The Show Tool Tips checkbox must be turned on in the General Preferences for this "pause preview" to work.

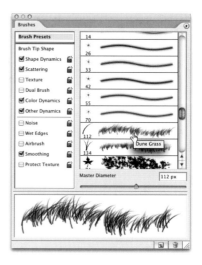

⬤ ⬤ ⬤ THE UNDOCUMENTED AIRBRUSH TOGGLE TRICK

This cool, undocumented shortcut comes from our good friend, Web wizard, and all-power-ful overlord of every Photoshop keyboard shortcut known to man, Michael Ninness (author of the book *Photoshop 7 Power Shortcuts*, from New Riders, ISBN 0735713316). Here's the tip: As you probably know by now, the Airbrush tool has been gone from the Toolbox since 7.0, but you can add Airbrush control to some painting tools by clicking on the Airbrush icon found in the Options Bar of most Brush tools. However, that takes a lot of trips up to the Options Bar. Ah, if only there were a keyboard shortcut that would let you toggle this Airbrush feature on and off at will. Well, there is, and thanks to Michael, we can share it here—it's Option-Shift-P (PC: Alt-Shift-P). Makes you want to buy Michael's book, doesn't it?

⬤ ⬤ ⬤ SWAPPING CROP FIELDS

Adobe snuck a little button into the Options Bar that's hardly noticeable. It works with tools such as the Crop tool (C), and it's a big time saver. For example, for the Crop tool it swaps the measurements in the Width and Height fields, so if you have the Crop tool set to crop to exactly a 5x7", if you click this Swaps button, it will now crop to 7x5". See? I told you it was handy.

Before

After

 **LET THOSE WINDOWS BREATHE!**

Since version 3.0, Photoshop has done something called "protecting the palettes" (I don't know if that's its official name, but we've always heard it called that). What it means is that as you increase the size of your image using the Zoom tool (Z), Photoshop stops increasing the size of the image window when it reaches the left edge of your open palettes (if you have turned on the Resize Windows To Fit checkbox in the Options Bar). When it reaches this safety zone, the window stops growing, and only the image within the window continues to zoom. The only way to get around this (in previous versions of Photoshop) was to close your palettes. Then you could zoom the window as large as you'd like. However, Adobe addressed this problem back in Photoshop 6.0, and now if you want to keep the window growing, choose Ignore Palettes in the Options Bar when using the Zoom tool.

 **THE MULTIPLE UNDO SHORTCUT**

Need to back up a few steps to readjust a setting? Piece of cake. Here's a shortcut to do just that. You can step back through your History palette (found under the Window menu) by pressing Command-Option-Z (PC: Control-Alt-Z) a few times. This doesn't delete the items, but takes you back a step in the History palette each time you apply the shortcut.

Before　　　　　　*After*

⬤ ⬤ ⬤ WANT ARROWHEADS? PHOTOSHOP CAN ADD THEM FOR YOU!

This one is pretty slick because it's been a feature in Photoshop for a while, but eight out of 10 Photoshop users will tell you Photoshop can't create arrowheads on the ends of lines (if it makes you feel any better, nine out of 10 dentists didn't think Photoshop could do it either). Here's how: First, go under the Shape tools (in the Toolbox) and choose the Line tool. Then, up in the Options Bar, you'll see icons for the Shape tools. Directly to the right of these eight icons is a down-facing triangle. Click on that triangle and out pops a dialog where you can click a checkbox to add arrowheads to either the beginning or end of your line, and you can choose the Width, Length, and even the Concavity (there's that dentist thing again).

⬤ ⬤ ⬤ DRAGGING-AND-DROPPING WHERE YOU WANT

If you drag an image from one document to another, the dragged image appears right at the spot where you let go of the mouse button. You may know that if you hold the Shift key when you drag-and-drop the image, the dragged image will automatically be centered within the receiving image. But you can go one better—make a selection in the receiving document, then hold the Shift key before you drag. Your image will be centered within the selection, instead of within the entire document. Scary, isn't it? You can also copy-and-paste the selection and Photoshop will center the pasted image in the selection.

⬤ ⬤ ⬤ FEATHER A SELECTION WITHOUT THE GUESSING GAME

Most of us try to guess how many pixels will give us the nice, soft selection we're looking for when we use the Feather Selection dialog (under the Select menu). Sometimes we guess right, and other times we press Command-Z (PC: Control-Z) to undo the damage before trying again. Try this instead: Make your selection first, and then press Q to turn on the Quick Mask mode. Now make the edge fade out by going under Filter, under Blur, and choosing Gaussian Blur. You can see how much of a blur you'll need to soften the edges as you adjust the Radius amount. When you're done, press Q to get back to Standard mode with the selection already made with the exact amount of feathering that you want.

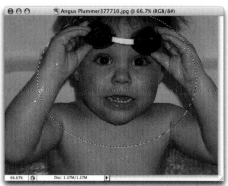

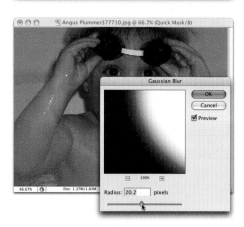

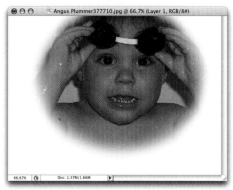

TOP-SECRET PHOTOSHOP SPLASH SCREEN

If you want to see the secret Photoshop beta startup screen (the pre-release version of Photoshop CS2), just hold the Command key (PC: Control key) and choose About Photoshop from the Photoshop menu (or Help menu on a PC). It will show you the splash screen, displaying CS2's secret pre-release code name. I'm telling you, those engineers know how to party.

FALL IN LOVE WITH A TEMPORARY BRUSH, OR NOT

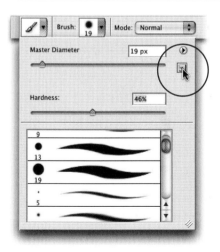

You can create a temporary brush anytime in Photoshop by playing with the options in the Brushes palette (which is nested in the Palette Well by default). After you make your choices, start painting. When you switch to another brush, the temporary brush you just created is gone. If you fall in love with your temporary brush (which is considered illegal in 48 states) and want to save it, before you change brush sizes, click on the Brush thumbnail in the Options Bar, and when the Brush Picker appears, click on the New Preset Brush icon in the upper right-hand corner, you sick pup.

UNDO A SAVE? THAT'S IMPOSSIBLE, ISN'T IT?

This is a great trick we learned from our buddy Mike Ninness, and the first time we saw it, we said, "Hey, wait a minute, that can't be." Uh, but it be. It's how to undo a Save. This is especially helpful after you've flattened an image, saved the file, then realized that you needed to change something on a layer. This only happens to us about every other day, and here's the keyboard

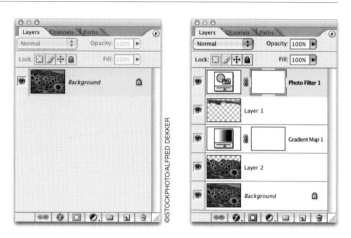

shortcut to fix it: Command-Option-Z (PC: Control-Alt-Z). Press it a few times after you've flattened and saved, and look in your Layers palette to see all the layers come a-rumbling right back. Pretty slick stuff.

CHANGE BRUSH SOFTNESS ON THE FLY

You can increase or decrease the softness of a round brush in Photoshop without changing the size of the brush by pressing Shift-Left Bracket or Shift-Right Bracket. That's almost too easy.

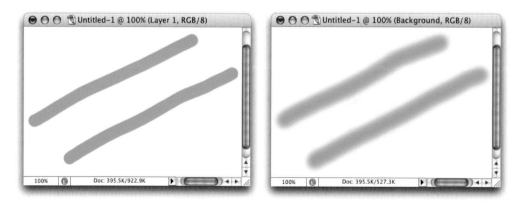

● ● ● HOW TO CORRECT ONE PROBLEM COLOR

Let's say you have an image, but the sky doesn't look as vibrant as you'd like, and you want to increase the amount of blue without affecting the rest of the image. Try this on for size: Open an image that contains a daylight sky. Click on the Create New Adjustment Layer pop-up menu at the bottom of the Layers palette and choose Color Balance. In the Color Balance dialog, drag the Blue slider all the way to the right (it looks bad now, but trust me) and click OK. Now, press B to switch to the Brush tool. Press the letter X until your Foreground color is black, and with a large, soft brush, start painting over the areas you don't want blue. As you paint, the blue Color Balance you added is painted away. The sky is much bluer, but you can paint away the added blue from the other areas. To really see the before/after difference, click the Eye icon next to the adjustment layer.

Before   *After*

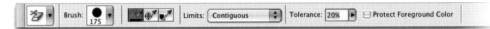

BUILDING A BETTER BACKGROUND ERASER TOOL

Here's a tip for making Photoshop's Background Eraser tool much more effective. Choose the Background Eraser tool (it's in the Eraser tool's flyout menu in the Toolbox), and in the

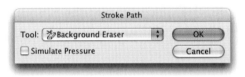

Options Bar, lower the Tolerance setting to 20%. Click on the Brush thumbnail to open the Brush Picker and choose a large, hard-edged brush. Then, press P to switch to the Pen tool, making sure that the Paths icon (middle one at left in the Options Bar) is selected. Draw a path just outside the edge of the object you want to isolate (you don't have to be precise; in fact, stay just outside the edges of the object and draw straight lines all the way around the image). Go to the Paths palette (under the Window menu), and in the palette's flyout menu, choose Stroke Path. When the dialog appears, under Tool, choose Background Eraser, and click OK. The Background Eraser will instantly trace around your image, following the path you created. Now that the edges have been erased, you can use the regular Eraser tool to erase the rest of the background area.

CUSTOM BRUSHES: START WITH A CLEAN SLATE

If you're going to build your own custom brush in Photoshop, sometimes it's easier to start with an existing brush and edit it. The problem is that you may have all sorts of settings already in place (Texture, Scattering, Shape Dynamics, etc., along with all their individual options). To set everything back to their defaults could take a while. At least it would if you didn't know this cool little trick: Click on the brush you want to use as your starting point for your custom brush, and in the Brushes palette, click on the options you want to edit (like Texture, Scattering, etc.). Then, from the palette's flyout menu, choose Clear Brush Controls, and all the selected options will be instantly reset to their default settings.

TIMING IS EVERYTHING!

Want to know how long a particular Photoshop command takes? Click on the right-facing triangle toward the bottom left-hand corner of your image window. From the pop-up menu that appears, under Show, choose Timing. This starts the equivalent of a stopwatch that times your Photoshop commands in seconds. This is great for speed tests, pitting one machine against another. Which one runs the fastest Smart Sharpen? Time it and find out.

Fast & Furious

CAMERA RAW TIPS

Hey there, it's me again (Felix). So here we are halfway through this book and Scott is having entirely too much fun writing these chapter intros. In fact, I just walked past his office

Fast & Furious
camera raw tips

and he was grinning from ear to ear. I asked what was so funny. He mumbled something about an old What's Happening!! *episode and how Raj, Dwayne and Rerun just crack him up. But I saw the chapter intro template on his PowerBook. I knew what he was up to.*

So, how can I best describe this chapter (before Scott discovers I snuck another one in while he's pretending to watch back-to-back episodes of Good Times, *and* Mama's Family*)? Well, it's like this. Imagine that Camera Raw is like* The Facts of Life. *You know, Tootie was the backbone of that show and Blair was simply riding her coattails after the second season. Sorry, I got sidetracked. The tips in this chapter are more like* Different Strokes. *You remember when Arnold would say, "What you talkin' 'bout Willis?" Now that was sitcom writing at its finest. Dang, I'm doing it again. Let me get back on track. OK, Camera Raw is really more like* Mork and Mindy. *Nanu-nanu is just another way to describe the histogram and how it... No, that's no good. I got it. Imagine you're Weezy, George Jefferson is the Metadata and Florence is like your digital camera's color space, and...*

⬤ ⬤ ⬤ **BLACK-AND-WHITE CONVERSIONS IN CAMERA RAW**

Believe it or not, Camera Raw is great for creating black-and-white conversions. Start by opening a RAW image, then lowering the Saturation to –100. Adjust the Exposure and Shadows sliders to create a nice contrasty image, then drag the Contrast slider to the right to give the image even more contrast. Now try all the different White Balance presets until you find the one that looks best for your particular conversion. You can even add sharpening if you like by clicking on the Detail tab and adjusting the Sharpness slider. And best of all, you can create a surprisingly good black-and-white image before it actually enters Photoshop CS2.

DON'T CLICK THE WHITE BALANCE TOOL ON SOMETHING WHITE

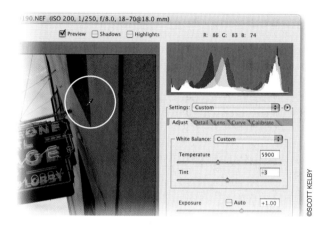

The White Balance tool (I) actually works best by clicking on something in your photo that is light gray, rather than clicking on something that is supposed to be white. Once you've clicked on a light gray area, use the Tint and Temperature sliders if you want to tweak the white balance a little bit, but use the White Balance tool to do most of the work.

UPDATING THE HISTOGRAM AS YOU CROP

The fact that Camera Raw has cropping built in should be cool enough, but its Crop tool (C) is smarter than Photoshop's. For example, when you drag out a cropping border in Camera Raw, take a look at the histogram in the top-right corner—it instantly updates to show you the histogram for *just* the areas that appear inside your cropping border. Sweet!

SLIDE AWAY THE ABERRATIONS

If you see areas of bright-colored fringe appearing around objects in your RAW photos, you're suffering from Chromatic Aberrations (well, you're not, but your camera's lens is). Under the Lens tab in Camera Raw, there are two sliders (Fix Red/Cyan Fringe and Fix Blue/Yellow Fringe) that let you slide those problems away, but seeing the problem clearly enough to eliminate the fringe is your first challenge. That's why you'll want to know this tip: If you hold the Option key (PC: Alt key) while you're dragging either Chromatic Aberration slider, it will only show the two channels you're adjusting in the preview area, making it easier to see—and repair—the problem.

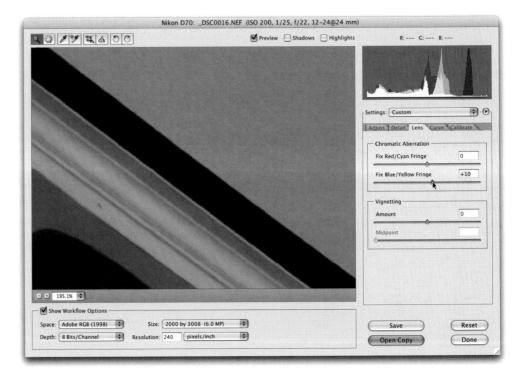

SEEING YOUR RAW IMAGE WITHOUT THE AUTO CORRECTIONS

By default, when you open a RAW image in Photoshop CS2, Camera Raw looks at the EXIF data embedded into your photo by your digital camera to find out which type of camera it was taken with, and once it knows, it applies a set of Auto corrections to the photo's exposure, shadows, brightness, and contrast. If you'd like to see what your RAW image looked like before Camera Raw applied these Auto corrections, just press Command-U (PC: Control-U), and it turns off all the Auto corrections to give you a clear, uncorrected view. Pretty bad, eh? So press Command-U (PC: Control-U) to turn those bad boys right back on.

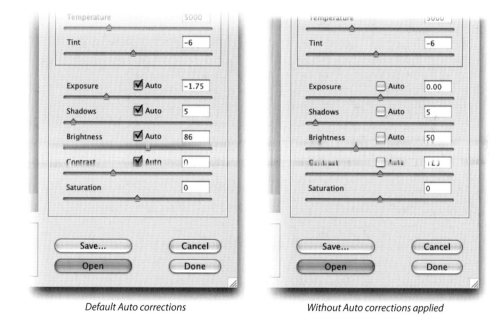

Default Auto corrections   Without Auto corrections applied

⬤ ◐ ◑ TOGGLING THE PREVIEW ON/OFF

So, have the adjustments you've made in Camera Raw helped or hurt your photo? Just press the letter P and you'll quickly find out. This turns the preview of your changes off, and shows how the original file looked before you started tweaking it. To turn the preview back on, just press P again.

©SCOTT KELBY

⬤ ◐ ◑ TURNING OFF AUTO CORRECTION FOR GOOD

If you don't like the Auto corrections that are applied to your RAW images by default, you can change things so that when you open photos from your camera, it will no longer perform any Auto corrections. Here's how: Open a RAW image and press Command-U (PC: Control-U) to turn off all the Auto corrections in Camera Raw. Then go under the flyout menu (to the right of the Settings pop-up menu) and choose Save New Camera Raw Defaults. Now, when you open a photo taken with the same camera make and model, it will no longer apply any of the Auto settings.

HOW TO UNDO THE WHITE BALANCE TOOL

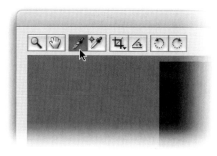

If you used the White Balance tool (I) to set the white balance in your image, and you don't like the results, you can undo your white balance setting by double-clicking on the White Balance tool in Camera Raw's Toolbox.

GETTING MORE READOUTS PER EYEDROPPER

In Photoshop CS2, the Color Sampler tool can give you readings from up to four different places, but the Color Sampler in Camera Raw is more powerful and monitors even more areas for you. Each time you click the tool, another set of readings appears at the top of the Camera Raw dialog, and although it looks like six is the maximum number of color samplers you can add to your image (because the top of the Camera Raw dialog looks full), you can actually add three more (for a total of nine color samplers). Try it, and you'll see the six samplers squeeze to accommodate three more samplers. Now, I have to say, if you need to monitor the color in nine different areas of your image, perhaps working with RAW images shouldn't be your biggest concern.

SHORTCUTS FOR HIGHLIGHT AND SHADOW WARNINGS

If you're going to be using CS2's new Highlight and Shadow clipping warnings, here are two shortcuts you'll need to know: Press the letter O to turn on the Highlight clipping warning (everything that appears highlighted in red is clipping), and press U to toggle on/off the Shadow clipping warning (everything that appears in blue is clipped to solid black with no detail).

CANCELLING A CROP IN CAMERA RAW

If you're using the Crop tool (C) in Camera Raw, and decide you want to cancel your Crop, just click on the Crop tool, then press the Escape key on your keyboard.

REMOVING A STRAIGHTEN IN CAMERA RAW

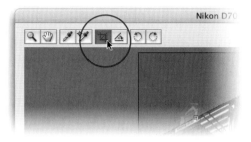

The Straighten tool (A) and the Crop tool (C) in Camera Raw are pretty much tied together. So much so, in fact, that if you want to cancel your straightening, you have to first click on the Crop tool (if it's not active by default after dragging with the Straighten tool), then press the Escape key on your keyboard.

HOW TO SEE THE SHARPENING NOW, BUT NOT APPLY IT

Many pros prefer to apply their sharpening in Photoshop itself, using Unsharp Mask or the Smart Sharpen filter, rather than in Camera Raw. If that sounds like you, wouldn't it be nice to just see what the sharpening would look like, even if you don't apply it? Of course, you could simply adjust the Sharpening slider (under the Detail tab) for a moment, look at the image, then slide it back—but there's a better way. While you have an image open in Camera Raw, press Command-K (PC: Control-K) to open the Camera Raw Preferences. When the dialog appears, change the Apply Sharpening To pop-up menu so it shows Preview Images Only. That way, any sharpening you apply in Camera Raw will only be applied to the preview you see onscreen in Camera Raw, and not the photo itself, so you can apply it later in Photoshop.

ADDING POINTS TO CAMERA RAW'S CURVE

Camera Raw in CS2 has its own curves adjust-ments (under the Curve tab), but adding a point to the curve is different in Camera Raw than it is in Photoshop. To plot a point on your curve in Photoshop, you just click the Eyedropper on the spot in your image you want plotted. But in Camera Raw, you have to Command-click (PC: Control-click) the Eyedropper instead.

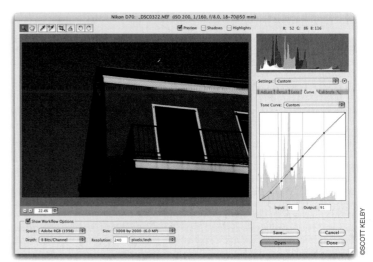

©SCOTT KELBY

SHORTCUT FOR ROTATING IMAGES IN CAMERA RAW

Save yourself a trip up to Camera Raw's Toolbox the next time you need to rotate an image. Just press L on your keyboard to rotate to the left or press R to rotate to the right. To rotate completely around, just keep pressing either letter.

CROPPING MULTIPLE RAW IMAGES AT ONCE

Want to crop just one RAW image and have that exact same crop applied to a number of similar RAW images at once? In Adobe Bridge, just Command-click (PC: Control-click) on all the RAW images you want to crop, then press Command-R (PC: Control-R) to open them in Camera Raw. Next, click the Select All button in the top-left corner of the Camera Raw dialog. Now press C to get the Crop tool, drag out your cropping border within the image in the preview area, and as you drag it out for the current photo, all the other selected photos will get the same cropping treatment, which will be reflected immediately in the list of images on the left side of Camera Raw.

LAST-MINUTE RENAMING IN RAW

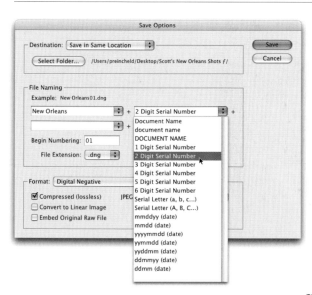

If you haven't renamed your photos, and you're busy processing them in Camera Raw, don't sweat it—you'll have an opportunity to rename them when you save them. In fact, when you choose Save in the Camera Raw dialog, the Save As screen that appears lets you batch rename the photos as they're saved. Just type the name you want in the first field, then the numbering scheme you want to use (after all, they can't all have the exact same name, right?).

BIGGER PREVIEWS IN CAMERA RAW

If you want a larger preview window in Camera Raw, you're only one click away. Just turn off the Show Workflow Options checkbox in the bottom-left corner of Camera Raw, and those options will be tucked out of sight, and your preview area will be expanded.

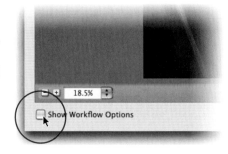

USE YOUR FAVORITE NAVIGATION SHORTCUTS IN CAMERA RAW

If you want to change the size of your preview window in Camera Raw, you can use most of the same keyboard shortcuts you already use in Photoshop. For example, to zoom in press Command–+ (Plus Sign) (PC: Control–+), and to zoom out press Command–– (Minus Sign) (PC: Control––). To jump to Fit on Screen view, double-click on the Hand tool. To jump to 100% size, double-click on the Zoom tool. To temporarily get the Hand tool, press-and-hold the Spacebar, then click-and-drag within the preview area.

MAKE IT ALWAYS FIT IN CAMERA RAW

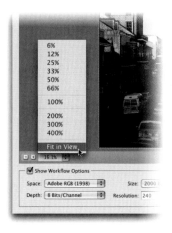

Here's a new viewing option—it's called Fit in View. It's found in the Zoom pop-up menu in the bottom-left corner of Camera Raw's preview window, and when you select it, it displays your entire photo as large as it can in the preview area.

HOW ABOUT A JPEG WITH THE RAW FILE? OH, A TIFF TOO?

If you decide that you want to create JPEGs from all your RAW images, the entire process is automated in CS2, but you don't do it from Camera Raw—you do it within Photoshop. You start by going under Photoshop's File menu, under Scripts, and choosing Image Processor. When the dialog appears, choose your folder of RAW photos, then choose the folder where you want the new JPEGs saved. In the third section, you choose the file type and the size you want your images to be. Do you want just JPEGs, or also TIFFs and PSDs as well? It's up to you. If you like, you can apply an action to your images and a copyright while you're at it. Once you've entered your preferences and clicked Run, Image Processor automatically creates separate folders (inside the folder you indicated in section two) for each type of file (JPEG, TIFF, or PSD).

DON'T CHANGE YOUR CAMERA'S COLOR SPACE FOR RAW

If you're shooting only in RAW (and not RAW+JPEG), then you don't have to worry about changing the color space in your digital camera to match the edit space in Photoshop. That's because you'll actually choose the color profile that will be assigned to the photo right before you process the RAW file—it comes in "untagged." It's RAW after all, right? So choose your color profile from the Space pop-up menu in the bottom-left corner of the Camera Raw dialog before you open the image in Photoshop. (*Note:* If you don't see the Space menu, turn on the Show Workflow Options checkbox.)

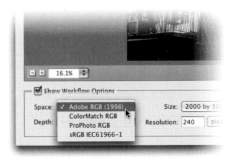

MAKING YOUR PHOTO BIGGER? DO IT IN RAW!

Another advantage of working with RAW images comes when you need to make your image larger than the original. Of course, this is generally thought of as a big no-no because making a photo bigger than its original usually means a major loss of sharpness and quality, but if you're shooting RAW, well...not

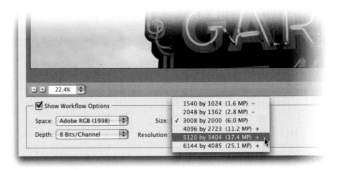

so much. Well, not nearly as much. So, all you have to do is go to Camera Raw's Workflow Options (in the bottom-left corner of the dialog), and from the Size pop-up menu choose a larger size (make sure you also choose 8 Bits/Channel for your depth), and you'll get much better results from your forbidden upsizing than you would have if you tried to do the same thing in Photoshop using the Image Size dialog (under the Image menu).

● ● ● HIDING YOUR METADATA FROM OTHERS

If you're providing photos to magazines, websites, or really just about anybody, you might want to strip out your metadata, or anybody with Photoshop will be able to learn a lot about you. For example, they'll know what kind of camera and lens you have (including make and model), what day you took the photo, edited the photo, and so on. Luckily, stripping the data out is easy, because you don't really strip it out. Just do this: Open the photo in Photoshop. Press Command-A (PC: Control-A) to select all, then press Command-C (PC: Control-C) to copy the photo into memory. Press Command-N (PC: Control-N) to create a new blank document in the same size, color mode, and resolution of your copied photo. Don't change anything; just click OK. When the new document appears, press Command-V (PC: Control-V) to paste your copied photo into your new document. Press Command-E (PC: Control-E) to merge this image layer with your Background layer, and save the file. The embedded EXIF data is left behind, giving you a clean image with no personal data attached.

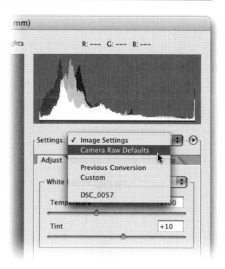

⬤ ◯ ◯ HOW TO GET BACK WHERE YOU STARTED IN CAMERA RAW

If you've made a number of adjustments in Camera Raw, and you're not happy with them and just want to get back to where you started, go to the Camera Raw Settings pop-up menu (it's just above the White Balance pop-up menu) and choose Camera Raw Defaults. That'll put the photo back to how it looked when you opened it.

⬤ ◯ ◯ BYPASS CAMERA RAW'S ANNOYING SAVE AS DIALOG

If you've been processing images and you want to quickly save a file with the settings you've just applied, you don't have to have the whole Save As dialog appear, which just takes up time and space. Instead, hold the Option key (PC: Alt key), and then click the Save button. It will simply save your image and apply the settings you selected without closing the Camera Raw dialog. It's faster, it's funner, and it's all gooder as well.

● ● ● SORTING IMAGES IN CAMERA RAW

When most of us think about sorting or rating images, we think about Bridge, but believe it or not, you can pretty much do the same thing right within Camera Raw. For example, let's say you open 60 images in Camera Raw. You can toggle through the different images by clicking on the left/right arrows in the bottom-right side of the preview window. To delete any image you don't like, click on the Trash icon in the Toolbox (it only appears when you have multiple images open). To add a star rating to a file, just click on it in the list of images on the left side of the dialog and drag out your rating below the image's thumbnail.

HAVING BRIDGE ALWAYS PROCESS YOUR RAW IMAGES

Double-clicking on a RAW image in Bridge opens that image in Photoshop's Camera Raw, but if you'd prefer to always have RAW images processed by Bridge's Camera Raw instead, just press Command-K (PC: Control-K) to open Bridge's

Preferences, and in the list on the left side of the dialog, click on Advanced. When the Advanced options appear, turn on the checkbox named Double-Click Edits Camera Raw Settings in Bridge.

HOW TO TELL CAMERA RAW WHICH PHOTO TO USE FOR EDITS

When you open multiple RAW images in Camera Raw, if you press Command-A (PC: Control-A) to select them all, any change you make to the top image in the list will be made to all the other selected images. But what if you'd prefer to edit the fourth or fifth image down, and have all the rest adjusted the same way (rather than having to adjust the first photo in the list)? It's easy—once all the photos are selected, Option-click (PC: Alt-click) on the photo along the left side that you want to base all your edits on. That photo will now appear in the preview window, and changes you make to it will also be applied to all other selected RAW photos.

LIKE THE EDITS YOU MADE TO ONE PHOTO?
APPLY THEM TO OTHERS

If you've got a number of photos open in Camera Raw, and you make some edits to one of those photos, and you think to yourself, "Hey, that doesn't look bad," you can quickly apply those same edits to other images. Here's how: Once you've made your edits to an image, Command-click (PC: Control-click) on the photos along the left side of the dialog to which you want to apply the same edits. Then click on the Synchronize button in the top-left side of Camera Raw. This brings up a dialog with a checkbox list of all the edits you can do in Camera Raw. If you want all the changes you applied to the first image to be applied to your selected images, choose Everything from the Synchronize pop-up menu at the top of the dialog. If you only want a few edits applied, uncheck the checkboxes beside the options you don't want.

REMOVING YOUR EDITS TO A RAW IMAGE IN BRIDGE

If you've edited a RAW photo in Camera Raw, you'll see a little round two-slider icon below the RAW photo's thumbnail in Bridge. If you want to remove those edits, and return the image to the original un-edited version (like it just came out of your camera), Control-click (PC: Right-click) on the thumbnail and choose Clear Camera Raw Settings.

CROPPING MULTIPLE IMAGES AT ONCE

If you've opened multiple images in Camera Raw, you can apply cropping to one of those images and then have that exact same cropping applied to as many other open images as you'd like, in just two clicks. First crop your selected image in the preview window using the Crop tool (C). Now select the other photos you want to crop by Command-clicking (PC: Control-click) on them in the list of open photos on the left side of the Camera Raw dialog. Then click on the Synchro-nize button. When the dialog appears, from the Synchronize pop-up menu at the top, choose Crop and click OK. All your selected photos will be cropped the same way you cropped the first photo.

I know I'm supposed to write something compelling to make you want to read this chapter, but honestly, they're layer tips. Not that they're unimportant—they totally are. But

Speedy Gonzalez
layer tips

when you say it—"layer tips"—it just doesn't have enough oomph! This chapter name needs more oomph! By the way, as an aside, if you look up the word "oomph" in the 2003 Webster's Abridged Dictionary, Oxford Version, for the actual definition, it's "a bulkiness or powerful quality that is brought on by most chapter heads, with the notable exception of 'Layer Tips.'" Hey, I'm not making this stuff up. Those Webster guys are serious (especially the one who had his own show and was friends with Michael Jackson).

FINALLY, A SHORTCUT FOR CREATING A FLATTENED LAYER

I'm not talking about flattening your image. I'm talking about a new layer that contains a flattened version of your whole layered document, without flattening your layers. That's right— one layer that looks like your flattened document. You could do this in previous versions, but it took a little doin'. Now, it's just one simple keyboard shortcut, and it even creates the layer for you—it's Command-Option-Shift-E (PC: Control-Alt-Shift-E).

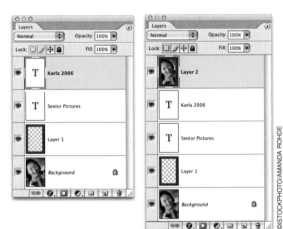

CHANGING OPACITY WHILE YOU'RE TRANSFORMING

Until CS2, this was impossible, but now when you have Free Transform active on a layer and you need to change the opacity of the layer you're transforming, you can do it by just going to the Layers palette and lowering the Opacity setting. But it's not just Opacity—you can change the blend mode as well. If you do photo restoration, or wind up having to take a head shot from one photo and composite it on another (the groom's eyes were closed, etc.), you know what a time saver this will be.

MOVING LAYER EFFECTS FROM ONE LAYER TO ANOTHER

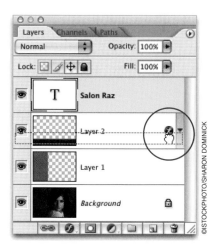

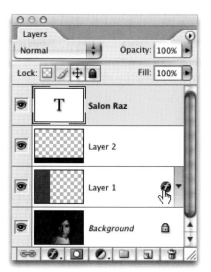

©ISTOCKPHOTO/SHARON DOMINICK

In previous versions of Photo-shop, when you wanted to move an applied effect (like a drop shadow or bevel and emboss) from one layer and have it appear on another layer, you'd copy the effect from your original layer, then paste it onto your preferred layer, then go back to the original layer and drag the effect into the Trash. Four steps are just too much. How about only one—just drag the little round "f" icon from the active layer to the layer you want it on, and it relocates to that layer. If you want to duplicate the effect (rather than move it), just Option-drag (PC: Alt-drag) the icon.

FASTER FLATTENING

In the past, if you wanted to flatten an image, there was only one way to do it—go to the Layers palette's flyout menu and choose Flatten Image. But in CS2, it's finally right at your fingertips. Just Control-click (PC: Right-click) on any image layer's name in the Layers palette and choose Flatten Image from the contextual menu that appears. It's not perfect, but it's faster than digging through the flyout menu. *Note:* The options in the contextual menu depend upon the type of layer on which you Command/Control-click.

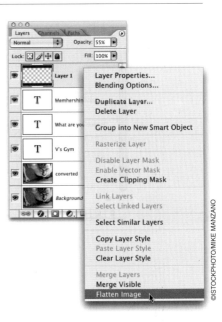

UNLINKING ALL YOUR LINKED LAYERS WITH A SINGLE CLICK

Here's another one we've been waiting (patiently, I might add) for a long time—the ability to unlink all your linked layers with a single click. Just click once on the Link icon at the bottom of the Layers palette and all layers linked to your current linked layer will be unlinked. See, if you just wait long enough….

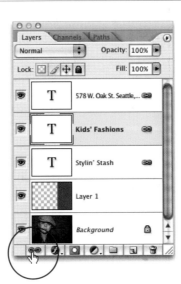

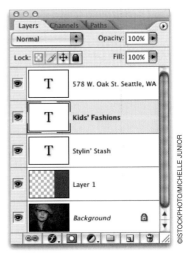

TEMPORARILY UNLINKING A LAYER

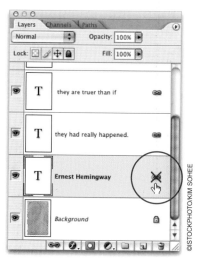

If you have a layer linked to another layer in CS2, you'll see a Link icon appear to the right of the layer's name (it appears there now, because the old Link column that used to appear to the left of layers is gone). If you hold the Shift key and click directly on that Link icon, that layer will be temporarily unlinked (you'll see a red X appear through that layer's Link icon). To relink it, just Shift-click on that icon again.

LOADING A LAYER SELECTION HAS CHANGED

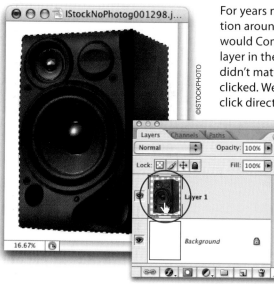

For years now, when you wanted to put a selection around everything on a particular layer, you would Command-click (PC: Control-click) on that layer in the Layers palette, and it pretty much didn't matter where you clicked, as long as you clicked. Well, in CS2, it matters. You now have to click directly on the layer's thumbnail to get the selection to load. So what happens if you Command-click (PC: Control-click) on the other part of a layer (the layer's name for example)? It highlights that layer, so you can select multiple layers at a time.

⬤ ⬤ ⬤ VISUAL CUES FOR A LAYER'S EDGE

Want to see where the edges of your current layer appear (especially handy if you're working with layers with soft edges)? Just go under the View menu, under Show, and choose Layer Edges. Now a thin blue border will appear around the edges of the currently selected layer to give you a visual cue of your layer's boundaries.

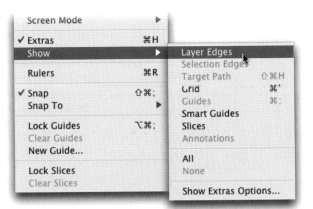

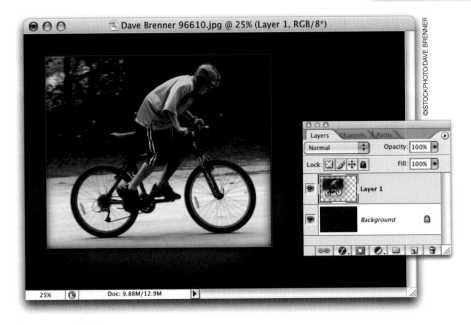

©ISTOCKPHOTO/DAVE BRENNER

DON'T WANT A GAP BETWEEN ITEMS? SNAP TO 'EM

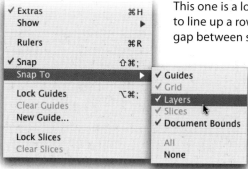

This one is a lot handier than it sounds. If you've ever tried to line up a row of objects, the last thing you want is a little gap between some of them (I just ran across this problem when I was trying to line up a row of television monitors for a video wall I was creating). Well, you don't have to have that gap anymore, because in CS2 you can actually have the layer you're moving snap right to the layer you're trying to align it to. Just go under the View menu, under Snap To, and choose Layers.

MOVING AND COPYING LAYER MASKS

If you wanted to move a layer mask from one layer to another, you used to have to jump through a few hoops, but in CS2 it's much easier. Just click directly on the layer mask's thumbnail and drag it to the layer where you want it. If you want a duplicate of a layer mask (rather than just moving it from one layer to another), press-and-hold the Option key (PC: Alt key) before you drag.

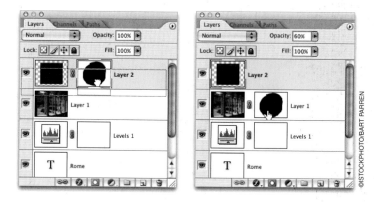

©ISTOCKPHOTO/BART PARREN

INVERTING A MASK AS YOU MOVE IT

This isn't a hard tip, but it's the kind of thing that only advanced users would want to do. It's the hidden shortcut for inverting a layer mask as you duplicate it (see what I mean)? Well, anyway, here's the tip: First hold the Shift key, then click-and-drag the layer mask thumbnail to the layer you want it to appear on. If you want to invert and duplicate the mask (rather than move it), hold the Option key (PC: Alt key) as well—so the shortcut is Option-Shift (PC: Alt-Shift) to duplicate and invert.

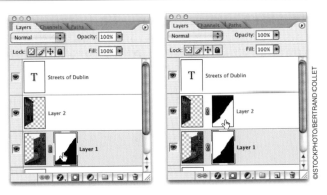

Here we duplicated and inverted the mask.

©ISTOCKPHOTO/BERTRAND COLLET

WANT TO "DRAG SELECT" LAYERS? YOU NEED TO TURN THIS ON

Although CS2 lets you "drag select" layers (and by that I mean you can drag out a selection around objects on layers in your document, and any layers your selection touches will become active in the Layers palette as if you linked them together), you have to know where to turn this feature on. First, press V to get the Move tool, then in the Options Bar turn on the checkbox for Auto Select Layer. Now, click-and-drag within your image and any layer that falls within your selection becomes active. Now you can move them as one unit.

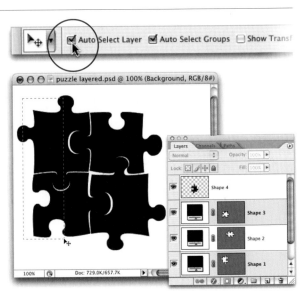

⊙ ⊙ ⊙ LAYER GROUP SUPER-SPEED TIP

Want a quicker way to create a Layer Group? Command-click (PC: Control-click) on all the layers you want to include in this new Group. Then press-and-hold the Shift key and click on the Create a New Group icon at the bottom of the Layers palette. This will create a brand new Group consisting of all of your linked layers.

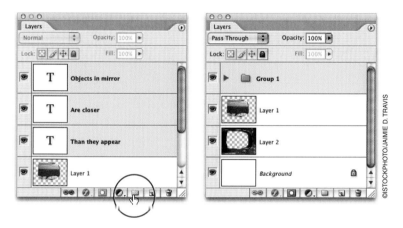

©ISTOCKPHOTO/JAIME D. TRAVIS

⊙ ⊙ ⊙ ALMOST A BUILT-IN FLATTENING SHORTCUT

I say "almost" because it works "almost" all the time. If you have a multilayered file and want to quickly flatten it, you can usually press Shift-Command-E (PC: Shift-Control-E). The only time it doesn't work is when you have a hidden layer, because what you're pressing is the new keyboard shortcut for Merge Visible. If all your layers are visible, it flattens them, but if even one layer is hidden, it won't merge all the layers, only the visible ones. So you can use this "almost" all of the time.

JUMP TO ANY LAYER JUST BY CLICKING IN YOUR IMAGE

You can jump to any layer in your document without going to the Layers palette. Press V to switch to the Move tool. Now, press-and-hold the Command key (PC: Control key), and click on an object in your image that you want, and you'll instantly jump to that object's layer.

TURNING YOUR LAYERS INTO SEPARATE DOCUMENTS

If you have a multilayered document and want to turn each layer into its own separate document, just go under the File menu, under Scripts, and choose Export Layers To Files.

Import	▶
Export	▶
Automate	▶
Scripts	▶
File Info...	⌥⇧⌘I
Page Setup...	⇧⌘P
Print with Preview...	⌥⌘P
Print...	⌘P
Print One Copy	⌥⇧⌘P
Print Online...	
Jump To	▶

Export Layers To Files
Image Processor
Layer Comps To Files
Layer Comps To PDF
Layer Comps to WPG
NAPP PDF Presentation with File Names

Script Events Manager

Browse...

OPENING LAYERED FILES WITHOUT ALL THE LAYERS

If you have a large multi-layered file, you know it can take a while to open, and that's fine—it's part of working with large files. But sometimes you're not going to actually work on the file, and you just want to open it, take a quick look at it, and then close it (maybe you just want to see if it's the version of the file you're looking for). So why waste time opening a huge multilayered file if you just want to take a quick look? Well, you don't have to—just go under the File menu, choose Open, and navigate to the layered file, but before you click the Open button, hold Option-Shift (PC: Alt-Shift). By holding those two keys down before you choose Open, it opens a flattened version of your layered file. Pretty darn slick.

MISSING YOUR BACKGROUND LAYER? HERE'S THE FIX

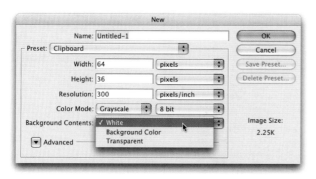

If you're opening new documents and they don't have a Background layer, there's a reason (of course there's a reason, everything has a reason; we just happen to know what it is). The reason is that you've selected the Transparent option in the New document dialog. That seems like a reasonable thing to do; everybody wants transparency, right? However, what it tells Photoshop is "Don't worry about creating a Background layer." To get Background layers again, the next time you're in the New dialog, under Background Contents, make sure you choose White, and from then on, you'll have Background layers in your documents.

AVOIDING THE LAYER MENU

Once you've applied a layer style to a layer, if you need to access some related commands that are in the Layer menu, you don't need to go up to the menu bar and go digging through the submenus. Instead, Control-click (PC: Right-click) on the little "ƒ" icon that appears to the right of your layer's name in the Layers palette. A contextual menu will appear with most of the Layer Style menu commands right at your fingertips—without the searching and digging through menus.

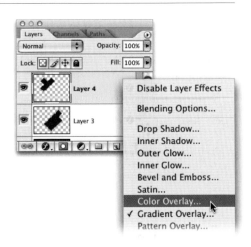

LOCK ALL THOSE LAYERS IN JUST ONE CLICK

You can lock all of your linked layers at once by choosing Select Linked Layers from the Layers palette's flyout menu, then choosing Lock Layers from the same menu. They'll kick and scratch for a while, but they'll eventually calm right down.

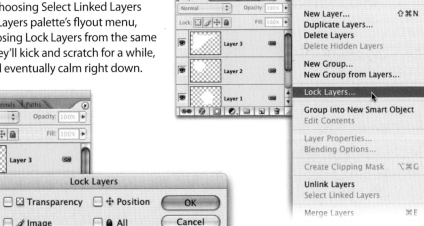

TOGGLE THROUGH THE BLEND MODES

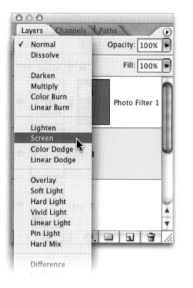

When I'm struggling to get just the right effect by changing the layer blend modes, it's great to be able to rotate through each mode without having to go back to the layer blend mode pop-up menu every time. To do this, simply switch to the Move tool (V), then press Shift–+ (Plus Sign). Every time you press it, it goes to the next blend mode.

HIDE YOUR OTHER LAYERS IN THE BLINK OF AN EYE

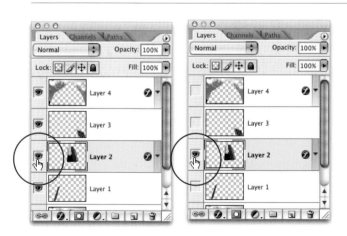

To hide an individual layer, click on the Eye icon in the first column next to that layer in the Layers palette. To make the layer visible again, click on the spot where the Eye icon used to be. If you want to keep one layer visible and hide all the others, hold the Option key (PC: Alt key) and click on the Eye icon beside the layer you want to keep visible. To make the other layers visible again, repeat the process.

WHY DRAGGING-AND-DROPPING STYLES ROCKS!

You probably already know that you can apply styles to an image from the Styles palette, and you may even know that rather than just clicking on them, you can drag-and-drop these styles right from the palette straight onto your current layer. But what's the advantage of dragging-and-dropping? Isn't it actually harder to drag-and-drop, rather than just clicking once? The advantage is that you can drag-and-drop styles to any layer, not just your currently active layer. You can also drag-and-drop effects between different open documents (like we did here).

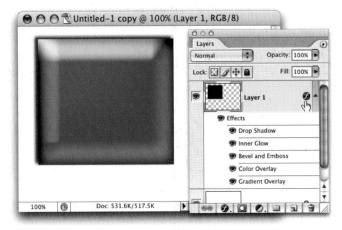

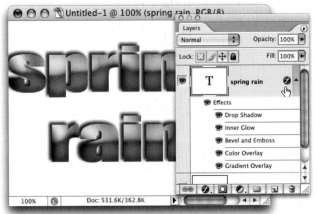

APPLYING LAYER STYLES TO YOUR BACKGROUND LAYER

How do you apply a layer style to your Background layer? You can't. That is, unless you double-click on your Background layer. This brings up the New Layer dialog where you can rename your Background layer, and when you do, it turns into a regular layer. Now you can apply layer styles to your heart's content. Want an even faster way? Just hold the Option key (PC: Alt key) and double-click, then you won't get the dialog at all—it will just convert it into a new layer named Layer 0.

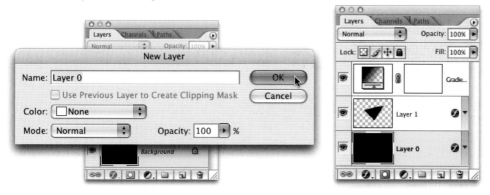

TURN YOUR LAYER COMPS INTO THEIR OWN DOCS

If you're using layer comps to compare different layouts within the same image, you can share these comps with people not on your network (or without access to your computer) by creating a separate document for each layer comp. This makes it easier to email them, and easier for your recipient to view them. Luckily, you don't have to do this all manually; just go under the File menu, under Scripts, and choose Layer Comps To Files.

⬤ ⬤ ⬤ MORE CONTROL OVER BLENDS: ADVANCED BLENDING

Using blend modes is a great way to get the layer you're on to interact with the layers beneath it. The only problem is you don't have much control over these blend modes— they either look the way you want them to, or not. They're pretty much an "on" or "off" tool. If you're looking for that next level of control over how layers interact with each other, you need the advanced Blending Options. These are found by double-clicking in the empty space just to the right of the layer's name in the Layers palette. What appears onscreen looks like the Layer Style dialog (and in fact, it is), but if you look closely, you'll see two bars with sliders at the bottom of the dialog giving you control over how your layered images interact. Here's another quick tip: If you hold the Option key (PC: Alt key) before you drag one of the sliders, it will split the slider in two, which gives you smoother transitions and more usable blend effects.

INSTANT OPACITY CHANGE

Anytime you want to change the Opacity of the layer you're currently working on, just switch to the Move tool (V) and press a number key on your keyboard: 4 = 40% Opacity, 5 = 50% Opacity, etc. If you want an exact percentage, such as 52%, then type 52. (*Note:* You have to type quickly, or you'll get 50%, then 20%.)

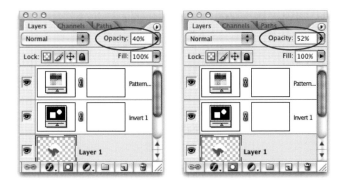

COPY A LAYER IN THE SAME LOCATION IN ANOTHER DOCUMENT

To make a copy of your current layer and have it appear in the exact location in a different Photoshop document, Control-click (PC: Right-click) on the layer in the Layers palette that you want to copy, and choose Duplicate Layer. When the Duplicate Layer dialog appears, choose the Destination from the Document pop-up menu, and click OK.

MOVING MULTIPLE LAYERS FROM DOCUMENT TO DOCUMENT

Want to move more than one layer at a time from one document to another? It's easy, as long as you know where to drag from. First, Command-click (PC: Control-click) to select your layers and then click the Link icon at the bottom of the Layers palette to link your layers together. Then, make sure that you drag your layer from within your document itself, rather than trying to drag the layer from the Layers palette. Dragging a layer from the Layers palette to another document is fine, as long as you only want to drag one layer at a time.

CENTERING DRAGGED LAYERS THE EASY WAY

When dragging a layer from one document to another, the object will appear in the new document at the point where your cursor was when you released the mouse button. If you'd prefer that the layer appear perfectly centered within the other document, just hold the Shift key as you drag, and when you release the mouse button, the object will be perfectly centered.

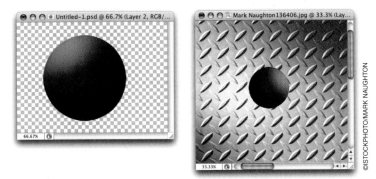

©ISTOCKPHOTO/MARK NAUGHTON

EASIER DROP SHADOW ANGLE ADJUSTMENTS

If you're creating a drop shadow using Photoshop's built-in layer styles (from the Add a Layer Style pop-up menu in the Layers palette), rather than setting the Distance and Angle numerically, you can adjust it visually. Just move your cursor outside the dialog right into your image, click on the shadow itself, and drag it where you'd like it.

LAYER NAVIGATION SHORTCUT

If you're working on a large, multilayered document and you have the Move tool (V) active, you can jump to the layer you want by Control-clicking (PC: Right-clicking) on a portion of the image. A contextual menu will appear with a list of the layers beneath the point where you clicked your cursor. To make one of those layers the active layer, just choose it from the menu. It's important to note that if there aren't any layers beneath where you're clicking (or the layers are transparent where you're clicking), the only layer that will appear in the menu is the Background layer.

SEPARATION ANXIETY: PUT A LAYER STYLE ON A SEPARATE LAYER

When you apply a layer style to a layer using the Add a Layer Style pop-up menu in the Layers palette, you've done just that—applied a style to a layer, and that style is married to that layer. However, if you'd like to edit your effect separately from the layer, you can ask Photoshop to put the layer style on its own separate layer (or layers if necessary). To do this, click on your layer, then go under the Layer menu, under Layer Style, and choose Create Layer. Your effect will now appear on its own layer beneath your current layer. *Note:* If you apply a bevel effect, it will create multiple separate layers.

LAYER EFFECTS REMOVAL SPEED TIP

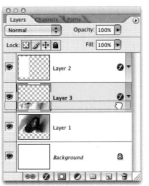 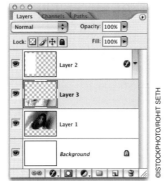

©ISTOCKPHOTO/ROHIT SETH

If you want to remove all the layer effects applied to a particular layer, don't drag them all into the Trash one by one. The fastest way is to simply drag the Layer Effects icon (it looks like a little "*f*") directly into the Trash icon at the bottom of the Layers palette, and all the effects go right along with it.

SHAPES WITHOUT THE SHAPE LAYER

If you use Photoshop's Shape tools, by default they create a Shape layer (which is basically a layer filled with your Foreground color with a clipping path in the shape of your shape, if that makes any sense). We've had loads of email from users asking us, "Do I have to have that funky Shape layer? Can't I just have the shape without the layer and clipping path?" Absolutely! When you choose one of the Shape tools, look in the Options Bar and on the far left you'll see three icons. Click on the third icon from the left and you'll get just the shape—no Shape layer, no paths, no kidding.

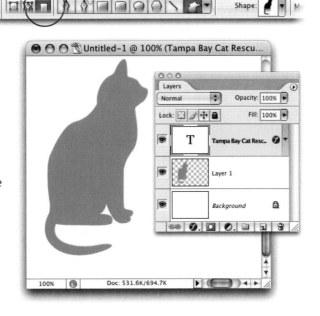

COLOR-CODING MADE EASY

In Photoshop you can color-code layers and layer sets for quick visual identification. One way to do this is to bring up the Layer Properties dialog (from the Layers palette's flyout menu) and choose your colors from a pop-up menu. But there's a much faster way—at least if you know this shortcut: Control-click (PC: Right-click) on the Eye Icon next to the layer you want to color-code and a contextual menu of colors will appear where you can choose the shade you'd like.

SPEED UP PHOTOSHOP BY MERGING LAYERS

Every time you add a layer to Photoshop, it adds quite a bit of file size to your image. The larger your file size, the slower Photoshop goes. If you're creating a document that has lots of layers, before long, your file size is going to get pretty huge. One way to keep things lean and mean is to merge any layers that don't need to be separate. You do this by clicking on the top-most image layer in the

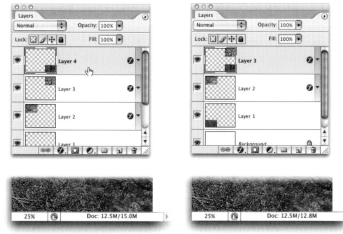

©ISTOCKPHOTO/RANDALL CHET

Layers palette, and then pressing Command-E (PC: Control-E). This merges the current layer with the layer directly beneath it. Think of it this way—every time you merge two layers, your file size drops and Photoshop gets faster. It's like a keyboard shortcut that adds more horsepower. *Note:* If one merge doesn't drop your file size, try merging again.

CAN'T WE ALL JUST HAVE THE SAME STYLE?

Want to apply a style that's on one layer to a bunch of other layers? It's easy (if you know the trick). Just link all the layers that you want to have that same style by Command-clicking (PC: Control-clicking) on them and clicking the Link icon at the bottom of the Layers palette. Then Control-click (PC: Right-click) on the layer's name with the style you want to copy and choose Select Linked Layers from the contextual menu that appears. Control-click (PC: Right-click) again and choose Paste Layer Style, and your style(s) will instantly paste to every linked layer.

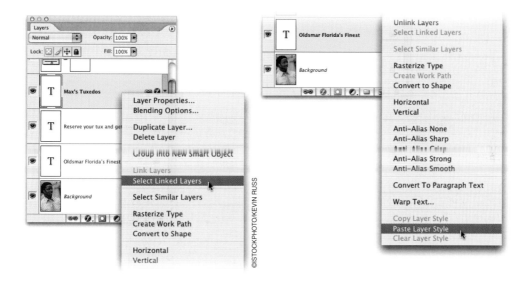

©ISTOCKPHOTO/KEVIN RUSS

⬤ ⬤ ⬤ LAYERS PALETTE NAVIGATION SPEED TIPS

The less you need to be in the Layers palette, the better (at least when it comes to speed), so here are some shortcuts you'll want to know: When you want to select multiple layers, press Option-Shift-Left Bracket ([) (PC: Alt-Shift-Left Bracket) to select layers beneath your current layer. To select layers above your current layer, press Option-Shift-Right Bracket (]) (PC: Alt-Shift-Right Bracket). To move your current layer down one layer at a time, press Command-Left Bracket (PC: Control-Left Bracket). To move it up one layer at a time, press Command-Right Bracket (PC: Control-Right Bracket). To switch to the layer beneath your current layer, press Option-Left Bracket (PC: Alt-Left Bracket). To switch to the Layer above your current layer, press Option-Right Bracket (PC: Alt-Right Bracket). To move your

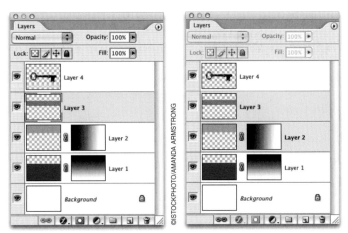

Here we selected the next layer down.

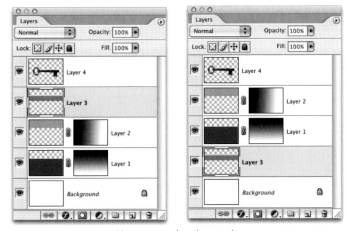

Here we moved our layer to the bottom of the layer stack.

layer to the top of the layer stack, press Command-Shift-Right Bracket (PC: Control-Shift-Right Bracket). To move your layer to the bottom of the layer stack (above your Background layer), press Command-Shift-Left Bracket (PC: Control-Shift-Left Bracket). Trust us, it's worth memorizing this stuff.

VIEW YOUR LAYER MASK AS A RUBYLITH

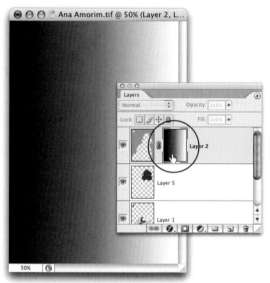

If you want to view your layer mask by itself (rather than how the layer mask affects your overall image), hold the Option key (PC: Alt key) and click directly on the layer mask thumbnail in the Layers palette. This will display just the mask itself. You can also view the layer mask like a Rubylith (a red overlay used in traditional masking) that appears over your image by pressing the Backslash key (\) on your keyboard.

CHAPTER 6 • Layer Tips   **143**

SELECTING JUST ONE OBJECT ON A LAYER

If you have multiple objects on the same layer (like a few words of type that have already been rasterized) and you want to select just one item on that layer (for example, you want to put a selection around one letter so you can move it independently of the rest of the letters), here's how: Use any selection tool to create a loose selection around the object. Hold the Command key (PC: Control key), and then press the Up Arrow key once and the Down Arrow key once. The entire object will become perfectly selected without disturbing anything else on the layer. Now you can move it, edit it, or tweak it separately because it is a "floating selection."

UN-FILLING FOR FUN AND PROFIT

Back in Photoshop 7.0, Adobe brought a once-buried command front and center when they added the Fill option to the Layers palette. This isn't your average everyday fill. No sir, this is a special freaky fill that only works when you've applied a layer style to a layer. To see it in action (and immediately understand its power), create some text, and then apply a drop shadow. Lower the regular Opacity of this layer, and you'll notice that both your type and the shadow fade at the same time. Now raise it back up to 100%. Then

lower the Fill amount (in the Layers palette) and you'll notice that the type fades away, but the drop shadow stays at 100%. Ahhhhhh. Makes you stop and think, doesn't it?

⬤ ⬤ ⬤ SECRET OPACITY SEE-THROUGH-PART-OF-A-LAYER TIP

This is a pretty wild tip—how to make just one part of a layer have a lower opacity. We know it sounds impossible, but this is totally cool. Start by making a selection on any area of the layer that you want to become transparent, while the rest of the layer remains at 100%. Then go under the Edit menu and choose Fill. When the Fill dialog appears, from the Mode pop-up menu choose Clear. Then lower the Opacity of the fill to whatever percentage you'd like, then click OK and voilà—part of your layer has opacity, while rest remains at 100%. Majorly cool!

(*Note:* You have to think in reverse here. Clear set to 100% Opacity will make the selected area completely transparent.) Wait, what if you decide later that you want to fill it back in? Here's how: Just start making copies of your layer by pressing Command-J (PC: Control-J), and as you do, you'll see the transparency disappear. You may have to make five or more copies, but son of a gun if it doesn't work. When it looks right, hide all but those copied layers, and from the Layers palette's flyout menu, choose Merge Visible.

©ISTOCKPHOTO/SANG NGUYEN

Do you remember the song "Burn Rubber" by the Gap Band from back in the early '80s? Remember it goes: "Burn rubber on me, Charlene… whoa, no…." Not ringing any bells?

Burn Rubber
smokin' type tips

It doesn't matter. This chapter has nothing to do with burning rubber—I was just curious to see if you're as old as I am (which is young. Very young. I heard that song accidentally on an oldies station in my dad's car). This chapter is dedicated to making the time you spend using type in Photoshop more productive. Here's the weird thing about Photoshop type—back in version 6.0, Adobe added most of the high-end typography features found in Adobe's high-end page-layout program, InDesign. Which made me think, "Why?" I can't imagine setting a book or magazine article in Photoshop, because when Photoshop type gets below 12 points, it starts to get fuzzy, so laying out columns of text and tweaking the balance, spacing, and paragraph specs for columns of type just doesn't make sense. Then I figured out what's going on. Somebody at Adobe must be hittin' the crack pipe. Could that be it? Or is it so not, that it freaks you out.

⬤ ⬤ ⬤ **BIGGER FONT PREVIEWS**

In Photoshop CS2, Adobe added font previews (where you can see a preview of how each font looks, right in the Font menu itself), but the previews are so small, it's still hard to tell the difference among fonts. Luckily, there is a way to make those previews large enough so they actually are usable—just press Command-K (PC: Control-K) to bring up Photoshop's Preferences, then press Command-9 (PC: Control-9) to jump to the Type preferences. In the Font Preview Size pop-up menu, choose Large, and now your font previews will be significantly larger.

⬤ ⬤ ⬤ **DON'T LIKE THE FONT PREVIEWS? TURN 'EM OFF**

I know everybody and their uncle has been waiting patiently for years to get font previews in the Font menu, but personally, they drive me nuts. Maybe it's the type freak in me that has led me to memorize what my favorite installed fonts are, but whatever it is, I hate seeing those previews (plus, it does slow the Font menu down a bit), so I turn it off. If you have the same level of disdain that I do for font previews, here's how to turn them off: Press Command-K (PC: Control-K) to bring up Photoshop's Preferences, then press Command-9 (PC: Control-9) to jump to the Type preferences. Now turn off the checkbox next to the Font Preview Size pop-up menu, and they're wiped from your Font menu.

CLICKING WITH THE TYPE TOOL TRICK

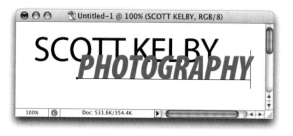

Here's one I learned from my buddy Matt Kloskowski, and it's something that has been driving me crazy for years, and I had no idea there was a way around it. It happens when you've already got some Type layers in your document, and you want to create some new type. When you click the Type tool (T) within your document, if you're anywhere in the vicinity of any other type, Photoshop thinks you want to add to that type (rather than creating some new type), so it puts your cursor in with your existing Type layer. Arrrrrggghh! Here's how to get around it—just hold the Shift key before you click the Type tool, and it ignores any nearby Type layers, letting you create a brand new string of type. Thanks to Matt for keeping me (us) from standing out on a ledge somewhere.

GETTING TYPE IN A PERFECT CIRCLE

Now that Photoshop can really give you type in a circle, getting a perfect circle that you can add type to is not as obvious as you'd think. To get this perfect circle, click on the Shape tools in the Toolbox and choose the Ellipse tool from the flyout menu (or press Shift-U). Then go up to the Options Bar, and in the group of three icons from the left, click on the middle icon, which creates a regular path, rather than a Shape layer or a pixel-based shape. Then, press-and-hold the Shift key, and drag out your circle (the Shift key constrains the shape to a perfect circle). Now you can press T to switch to the Type tool and move your cursor over the circle. When it changes into a Type on a Path cursor, click on the circle and get to typin'.

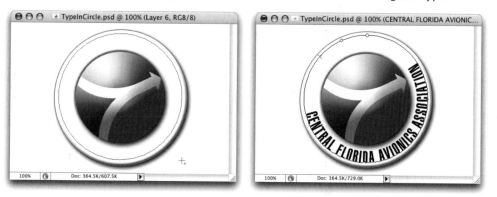

● ● ● I NEED MY DUMB QUOTES AGAIN

In all previous versions of Photoshop, when you typed in a quote mark (") or apostrophe ('), what Photoshop gave you was the typographically incorrect inch mark (") or foot mark (') instead. They're called "dumb quotes." Luckily, back in Photoshop 7.0, Adobe brought these typographically challenged dummies into line, and now they're properly applied as "curly quotes" by default, which is great. That is unless you have to actually type an inch mark or a foot mark. Here's the work-around—when it comes time to type an inch or foot mark, go under the Photoshop menu, under Preferences, and choose Type (in Windows, Preferences can be found under the Edit menu). In the resulting dialog, turn off Use Smart Quotes, and then type your characters. When you're done, return to the Type Preferences and turn them back on to bring typographic order to your world.

● ● ● RESETTING YOUR TYPE

If you're into typography, Photoshop gives you loads of typographical control. You can adjust everything from tracking, kerning, and dozens of other character-istics. The downside is—the Character palette (where we make most of these tweaks) keeps your last-used settings as a default. If you did some major type tweaking to your last line of type, it might need some major "undoing" in the Character palette to get you back to normal type settings. Rather than manually resetting every field, you can quickly reset Photoshop's type to its "default" standard settings by going to the Character palette and choosing Reset Character from the palette's flyout menu.

ONE-CLICK ACCESS TO THE COPYRIGHT SYMBOL, AND MORE

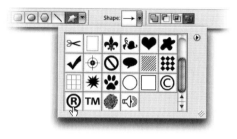

Looking for some special type characters, like ©, ™, or ®? If you're not fussy about these characters not actually being a font, you can find them in the default set of Custom Shapes. Just get the Custom Shape tool (press Shift-U until you have it), click on the Shape thumbnail in the Options Bar, which opens the Custom Shape Picker, and you'll find all three special characters there, in the default set of shapes.

HIGHLIGHTING YOUR TEXT SUPER FAST!

When you want to automatically highlight the type in a Type layer *and* switch to the Type tool at the same time to make some copy changes, just double-click directly on the "T" thumbnail on the Type layer you want to edit in the Layers palette, and blam! You're ready to go.

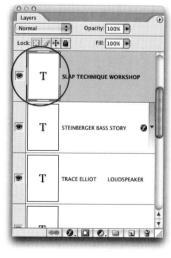

RENDERING TEXT IN JUST ONE CLICK

If you need to convert your Type layer into an image layer, you can save some time by simply Control-clicking (PC: Right-clicking) directly on the Type layer name that appears in the Layers palette. A contextual menu will appear where you can choose Rasterize Type to instantly render your type.

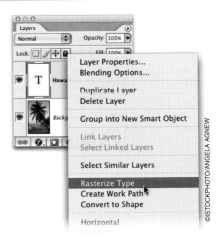

MADE TO FIT

To create a text box for your type to fit within, press T to select the Type tool, then click-and-drag out the area you want for your text box. Your type will now fit within that box. When you're finished entering your text, just press Enter on your numeric keypad (or Command-Return [PC: Control-Enter] on your laptop) to get out of the text bounding box.

TEXT-PATH-MAKING MANIAC

If you want to convert your Type layer into paths (as if you meticulously drew the type with the Pen tool—your clients won't have to know), simply go under the Layer menu, under Type, and choose Create Work Path.

PICTURE THIS: PUTTING A PHOTO INSIDE TYPE

First, set your Foreground color to black by pressing D. Press T to choose the Type tool and create your text (you don't have to rasterize the type). Then, open the image you want to appear inside your type and use the Move tool (V) to drag-and-drop it into your type document (it should appear on the layer above your Type layer. If it doesn't, just go to the Layers palette and move it on top of your Type layer). To put your image inside the type, press Command-Option-G (PC: Control-Alt-G) to create a clipping mask and whammo—your image is masked into your type. You can reposition the image by using the Move tool. And since you didn't rasterize your Type layer, your text remains totally editable—just click on the Type layer and start editing. You can add layer styles to your Type layer to further enhance the effect. If you're not crazy about the image you picked, click on the image layer and press the keyboard shortcut again to release the mask. Now remove the image.

● ● ● FONTS, FONTS, AND MORE FONTS

Here's a tip to quickly change typefaces and see the change while you
make it. First, highlight the type
you want to change, and then press
Command-H (PC: Control-H) to hide
the highlighting (the type is still
highlighted; the highlight is just
hidden from view). Then, up in the
Options Bar, click once in the Font
field, then use the Up/Down Arrow
keys on your keyboard to scroll
through your installed typefaces.
Man, do I love this one.

⬤ ⬤ ⬤   MAKE YOUR TEXT JUMP INTO ACTION

Earlier, I gave you the quick tip for rasterizing your type by Control-clicking (PC: Right-clicking) on your Type layer in the Layers palette, then choosing Rasterize Type from the contextual menu that appears. Believe it or not, there's an even faster way, if you don't mind spending a minute or two setting it up. You can create an action that rasterizes the type for you with just one key. Here's how: Use the Type tool (T) to create a Type layer, then make the Actions palette visible (from the Window menu). Choose New Action from the Actions palette's flyout menu. Name your new action "Rasterize Type Layers," assign it an action set from the Set pop-up menu, then from the Function Key pop-up menu, assign an F-key to this action. Click the Record button, then go under the Layer menu, under Rasterize, and choose Type. Now go back to the Actions palette and click on the Stop icon at the bottom of the palette (it's the first icon from the left). That's it—your action is written. Test it by creating a Type layer, then pressing the F-key you assigned to your action. It should instantly rasterize (you'll know if it worked, because the "T" icon on the Type layer will no longer be visible).

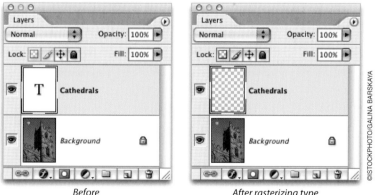

Before   After rasterizing type

⬤ ⬤ ⬤   DOUBLE YOUR PLEASURE

We've already talked about rasterizing
text, but once you've rasterized your
Type layer into a regular image layer,
your type is no longer editable (meaning you can't go back and change
typefaces, type in a different word,
adjust leading or kerning, etc.). Here's
a quick way around that limitation.
Before rasterizing (rendering) your type,

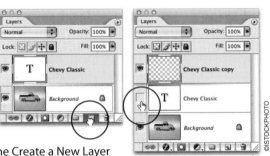

duplicate the Type layer by dragging it to the Create a New Layer
icon at the bottom of the Layers palette. Then, hide the original
Type layer from view (by clicking on the Eye icon next to the original Type layer) and rasterize
the duplicate Type layer (see previous tip). That way, if you ever need to go back and change
the word (or font, leading, etc.), you have the original editable Type layer still available. Just
simply make it visible by clicking in the empty box where the Eye icon used to be.

⬤ ⬤ ⬤   MOVE YOUR TYPE, WITHOUT SWITCHING TOOLS

Here's a tip that can save you a lot of tool switching when formatting your type. Once you
create your type with the Type tool (T), and while your cursor is still blinking somewhere
in the text, if you need to move the type, you don't have to switch to the Move tool—just
move your Type cursor away from your type (either above, below, or an inch or so to the
right or left), and your cursor will temporarily change to the Move tool. You can now simply
click-and-drag your type. If you want to edit your type some more, just move your cursor
back to the type and click where you need to make edits.

⬤ ⬤ ⬤ SEEING YOUR TYPE CHANGE COLOR

In Photoshop, you can change the color of your type without even selecting it first. "Why is that important?" you may ask. If you highlight your type to change its color using the Foreground color swatch in the Toolbox, the highlighting hides the color of your type so you can't see any of your color changes while you're in the Color Picker. So instead, after you commit your type by pressing the Enter key, click on the Color swatch in the Options Bar (without highlighting your type first) when you have the Type tool (T) active. As you change colors in the resulting Color Picker, you'll see your type update on the fly.

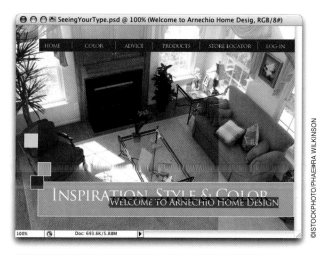

EDITING TEXT WITHOUT HIGHLIGHTING IT

Here's a cool little tip for changing your text without having the Type tool active. Just click on your Type layer (in the Layers palette), then go under the Window menu and choose Character. When the Character palette appears, you can make changes to your type size, color, font, tracking, etc. It freaks you out, doesn't it?

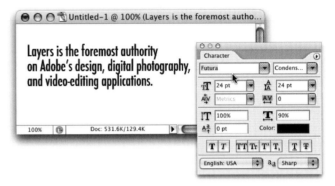

RASTERIZE TIMES 2, 4, 6...

If you have multiple Type layers and you want to convert them all to image layers, there's a way to do it without individually rasterizing each. Simply go under the Layer menu, under Rasterize, and choose All Layers. This will rasterize all the Type layers at once.

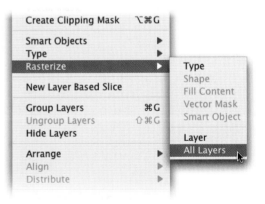

HONEY, I NEED SOME SPACE: VISUALLY ADJUST KERNING

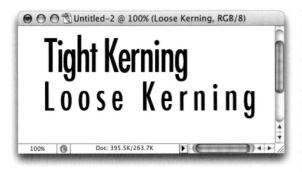

You can visually control the spacing between your type (which is much better than numerically trying to figure it out) by using the same keyboard shortcuts for adjusting type that Adobe Illustrator uses. Here's how: To set the tracking tighter (tightening the space between each letter or word in a group), highlight the type with the Type tool (T), then press Option-Left Arrow (PC: Alt-Left Arrow) to tighten. Press Option-Right Arrow (PC: Alt-Right Arrow) to add more space between a selected group of letters or words. To adjust the space between two individual letters (called kerning), click your cursor between the two letters and use the same keyboard shortcuts mentioned above.

TELL PHOTOSHOP WHEN YOU'RE DONE WITH TYPE

As you probably know, you can jump to most any tool in the Toolbox by pressing a single-key keyboard shortcut. (If you didn't know that, sell your copy of Photoshop. Kidding. Just turn to Chapter 2 for some essential tips.) Here's the problem: While creating type with the Type tool (T), if you press one of those one-key shortcuts (let's say the letter P for the Pen tool), instead of jumping to the Pen tool, Photoshop types the letter "p". It'll drive you nuts. Okay, you won't go nuts, but at the very least you'll have a lot of typos. The reason is this: You have to tell Photoshop that you're done editing your type. You do this in one of three ways: (1) Click on the checkmark icon at the far right of the Options Bar, (2) press the Enter key on your numeric keypad (or Command-Return [PC: Control-Enter] on your laptop), or (3) switch to another tool manually by clicking on it in the Toolbox. Any of these three tells Photoshop that you're done and lets you use the single-key shortcuts to switch tools.

BRING THOSE TYPE LAYERS TOGETHER

How do you merge two Type layers together? Unfortunately, while they're still editable Type layers, you can't—you have to rasterize the layers first. Technically, you rasterize just one (the bottom of the two Type layers), and then make the top Type layer active and press Command-E (PC: Control-E) to merge these two layers together. However, when you do that, the top Type layer will automatically rasterize as the two layers are combined into one, so there's really no way around it—with the exception of this little tip: Highlight the editable type on the top layer and choose Cut from the Edit menu. Switch to the lower Type layer, click your Type cursor once at the end of the type, press Return (PC: Enter) to start a new line, then choose Paste from the Edit menu to paste the contents of the top Type layer into the bottom Type layer. Then drag the old top Type layer into the Trash icon at the bottom of the Layers palette. Although it takes a little effort, now you have both layers combined into one layer (your goal), but the type remains totally editable (the bonus).

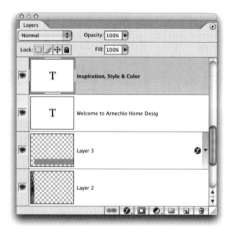
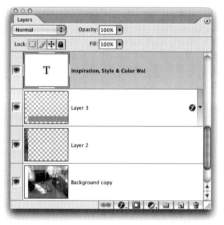

⬤ ⬤ ⬤ **THE LONG AND THE SHORT OF TYPE**

Although the Character palette has numeric controls for making your type fatter (horizontal scaling) or taller (vertical scaling), it's usually easier to do these two functions visually
(rather than numerically). Here's how: First set your type, then with the Type cursor still
blinking somewhere in the text, press-and-hold the Command key (PC: Control key) to
bring up the Free Transform bounding box. To make your type fatter, click on the center
(or corner) handle on either side, release the Command/Control key and drag outward. To
make your type taller, grab the center (or corner) handle on the top or bottom, release the
Command/Control key, and drag upward or downward.

⬤ ⬤ ⬤ **MADE TO FIT: PART TWO**

This tip relates to a previous tip, where you created what's called a "text box" so that your type wraps within a text block, rather than running in one straight line. The tip is this: If you've created some standard type by just clicking and typing rather than creating a paragraph text box, you're not out of luck. While the Type layer is active, just go under the Layer menu, under Type, and choose Convert to Paragraph Text. Now your type will wrap within the text box boundaries, and you can edit the boundaries by adjusting the corner and center points.

⬤ ⬤ ⬤ **MAKING THE SPELL CHECKER OBEY YOUR COMMANDS**

Photoshop's spell checker isn't just window dressing; it has a very robust spell-checking function, akin to Adobe InDesign's own spell checker, but if you understand how it works, you can save yourself some time and frustration. Basically, if you highlight some text on a layer, it checks just the highlighted text, so if you highlight one word, it just checks that one word (even if there are dozens of words in your paragraph). If you choose to spell check but don't have anything highlighted, it checks your entire document, regardless of how many Type layers you have. It's also helpful to know that it only checks real Type layers (layers that have a capital "T" as their thumbnail image in the Layers palette), and it cannot spell-check any layers with text that have been rasterized (converted from a Type layer into a regular image layer).

EDITING TYPE ON A PATH

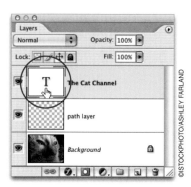

©ISTOCKPHOTO/ASHLEY FARLAND

If you've created some type on a path, highlighting that type to edit it (to change the font, color, spelling, etc.) can be kind of tricky. That's why it's quicker to go to the Layers palette and double-click directly on the "T" thumbnail icon. This will highlight all the type on this layer, making it easy to type in some new text, or change some of the attributes.

EXACT SIZING FOR YOUR TEXT COLUMNS

We already showed you how to create a column of type by clicking-and-dragging the Type tool to create your text box so your text will wrap within that column. But here's a quick little tip that lets you tell Photoshop exactly the width and height you'd like your type column to be (rather than just clicking-and-dragging it out visually). With the Type tool, just hold the Option key (PC: Alt key) and click in your document and the Paragraph Text Size dialog will appear where you can enter the exact size you'd like for your column.

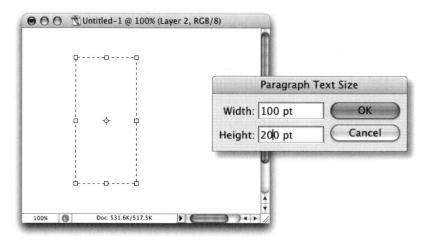

REMOVING THOSE TYPOGRAPHICALLY INCORRECT SPACES

If you're trying to set type that looks typographically correct in Photoshop, there's an old habit you'll have to break, and that's the curse of putting two spaces at the end of every sentence. This is a holdover from people who at one time used traditional typewriters, where adding two spaces was necessary, but in typesetting that's a huge no-no. About 70% of the text I copy-and-paste from text files that people give me has two spaces, but I use this Photoshop tip to fix the problem in just seconds. First, go under the Edit menu and choose Find and Replace Text. In the Find field, press the Spacebar twice (entering two spaces), then in Change To, press the Spacebar just once. Click Change All, and every time Photoshop finds two spaces at the end of a sentence, it will replace it with just one, making you typographically correct.

DON'T HAVE ITALIC OR BOLD? DON'T SWEAT IT

If you have a typeface that doesn't have a bold or italic version available, don't sweat it—Photoshop can make a fake bold or italic version for you. They're called faux bold and faux italic (don't pronounce them "fox bold" or the French will get really cranky about it. It's pronounced "fo," as in "Fe, Fi, Fo, Fum"). To apply a faux style to the type, highlight your type and choose Faux Bold or Faux Italic from the Character palette's flyout menu. Here's another tip: Don't forget to turn off these faux styles when you're done, because they don't automatically turn themselves off. Vive le Français!

TWEAK ALL YOUR TYPE WITH ONE FELL SWOOP!

This is a pretty darn slick tip for changing the font, size, or color of a number of different Type layers all at once. Here's how it's done: First, link all the layers that you want to adjust by Command-clicking (PC: Control-clicking) on each Type layer, then clicking on the Link icon in the bottom left corner of the palette. Linking the layers helps you keep track of your text. Now, just choose the Type tool (T) and go straight to the Options Bar or the Character palette. The change you make to one Type layer will also affect all the selected Type layers. The key is *not to highlight your type.* Schweeeet!

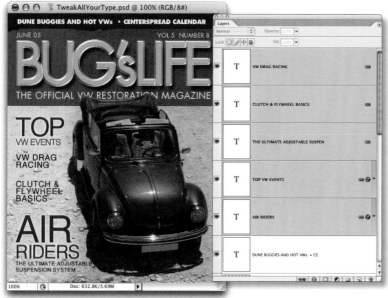

Speed Two

IMAGE CORRECTION AND PREPRESS TIPS

We're getting near the end of the book, and I'm growing tired. Dark figures dance across the windows like so many shadows gathering dust for the fall harvest (see, this is

Speed Two
image correction and prepress tips

why they don't let me write chapter intros at 2:30 a.m. anymore). Originally, this chapter was going to be a catchall chapter—a place for all those tips that couldn't find a home, but as luck would have it, we had so many image correction and prepress tips, they actually took over the catchall chapter by force. Now, because we stuck these tips toward the back of the book, does it mean that these tips aren't as good, aren't as important, or aren't as cool as the tips in all the other chapters? Yes, that's exactly what it means. These are the tips that just aren't worth a darn, so don't even waste your time reading them, because frankly, I'm not sure how many of them really work. Oh, I'm sure one or two do, but at this point, I'm just making stuff up. I know there are many new users of Photoshop that will be reading this book, so I think a description of the term "prepress" is in order. "Pre," as you know, means before, and "press" is derived from the Latin word meaning "to unwrinkle one's pants with an iron." So, basically, read this chapter before you wrinkle your pants.

HOW ACCURATE DO YOU NEED TO BE WHEN REMOVING RED EYE?

Not very. That's right, when you're using the Red Eye tool (Shift-J until you have it), you can click directly on the red that appears in the pupil, but if you're afraid that you won't be able to click directly

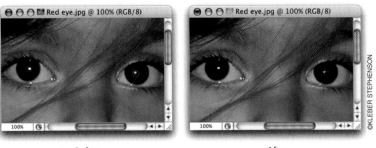

Before   *After*

©KLEBER STEPHENSON

on the red area (which can happen due to squinting, eye lashes, etc.), don't sweat it. Just click somewhere near where the red eye appears, and it will still remove the red eye. The tool is sensitive enough to search out any red that's even near where you clicked, so that's why the answer to the question "how accurate do you need to be when clicking?" is "not very."

GETTING BETTER SHADOW/HIGHLIGHT RESULTS

The Shadow/Highlight feature in Photoshop is pretty amazing, but as amazing as it is, sometimes opening up the shadows can give your photo a "milky" look to it, making it obvious that you made adjustments using Shadow/Highlight. Well, here's a tip for getting around that. First open Shadow/Highlight by going under the Image menu, under Adjustments, then choosing Shadow/Highlight. When the dialog opens, click on the Show More Options checkbox. Then, in the Shadows area up top, lower the Amount from the default setting of 50% to something more like 20%. Then increase the Tonal Width a bit and the Radius setting quite a bit, until the shadows are opened, but it doesn't look "milky" or over-processed. Once you've done this, you can slowly increase the Amount slider, but stop if it starts to look milky.

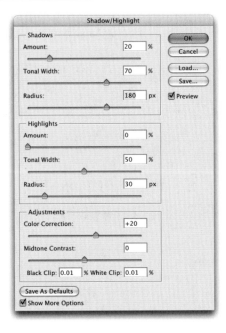

⬤ ⬤ ⬤ DITCH THE ANNOYING LENS CORRECTION GRID

I love the Lens Correction filter in CS2, but I dearly hate the grid that appears over every image every time I open one, and it's on by default, so you have to manually turn it off. However, if you're like me (and you know you are), and you want that grid off fast, there is a workaround—you can save your own custom setting with the grid turned off. But to do that, you have to change something (or the Save Settings will be grayed out). I found a workaround that has virtually no effect on your image. Open the Lens Correction filter (found under the Filter menu, under Distort), and then increase the Vignette Midpoint to 51% (a 1% increase). Then, at the bottom of the dialog, turn off the checkbox for Show Grid. Now, in the Settings flyout menu, you'll be able to choose Save Settings.

DETERMINING THE MOTION ANGLE IN SMART SHARPEN

Here's a tip I picked up from our buddy and NAPP Help Desk Director Peter Bauer. In Smart Sharpen (under Filter, choose Sharpen), there's a special form of sharpening that removes visible motion blur. This sharpening is called (are you ready for this?) Motion Blur sharpening, and you choose it from the Remove pop-up menu in the Smart Sharpen dialog. But here's the catch—you have to be able to determine the angle of the blur for Smart Sharpen to remove it. So, that's where Pete's tip comes in. You grab the Measure tool (nested under the Eyedropper tool in the Toolbox), and drag it along the angle of the blur. Then, look in the Options Bar and you'll see the angle degree listed after the letter A. That's the number you enter in the Motion Blur Angle field within Smart Sharpen. Very clever, Mr. Bauer.

©ISTOCKPHOTO/BILL GROVE

GETTING MORE ACCURATE COLOR USING REPLACE COLOR

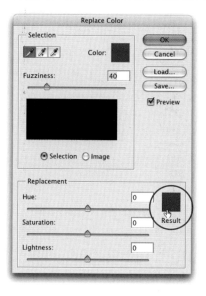

If you're using Replace Color (under the Image menu, under Adjustments) to select an area within your photo and replace it with a different color, the new color is pretty much an approximation, because you're dragging sliders, rather than inputting the exact RGB or CMYK build you're looking for. In Photoshop CS2, there's a way around this. Once you've selected the area of color you want to replace, click on the color swatch to the right of the sliders in the Replacement section (it wasn't there in previous versions). This brings up the Color Picker, where you can enter the exact RGB or CMYK values for your new color.

CORRECTING HIGHLIGHTS? WATCH OUT FOR OPEN SHADOWS!

If you open the Shadow/Highlight command (found in the Image menu, under Adjustments) to open up the shadows in your photo, you're in good shape from the get-go because it automatically increases the shadow area by 50%. That's great, if that's what you're after. But what if you're trying to pull back the highlights in a photo? Shadow/Highlight doesn't know that and by default still opens up your shadows by 50%. The way to combat this is to immediately drag the Shadows slider all the way to the left when the dialog appears, so now you can adjust (pull back) the highlights by dragging the Highlights slider to the right, which affects just the highlights and not the shadows.

HOW TO HEAL ON A BLANK LAYER

One of the cornerstones of professional retouching is to always perform your retouches on their own separate layer. That way you never "bruise" (damage) the pixels of the original image. However, when using the Healing Brush in Photoshop 7.0, you really had no choice—you had to use it on the same layer. In Photoshop CS2, you can heal to another layer. But first, there's a little setting you have to change. Get the Healing Brush from the Toolbox, then up in the Options Bar, turn on the checkbox for Sample All Layers. Next, click on the Create a New Layer icon at the bottom of the Layers palette to create a new blank layer above your Background layer and do your "healing" there.

BETTER HEALING WITH A CUSTOM BRUSH

I have to give credit for this incredible tip to NAPP member Stephanie Cole, who showed it to me after the Midnight Madness session at the Photoshop World Conference & Expo in LA. She pointed out how you can get a real mottled-looking result sometimes when using the Healing Brush. However, she found that when you change the brush shape (by clicking on the Brush thumbnail in the Options Bar) to a tall thin brush, it heals using a star-shaped stroke. This greatly reduces the mottling often associated with the Healing Brush, creating a smoother-looking, more natural retouch. My thanks to Stephanie for allowing me to share her very slick trick.

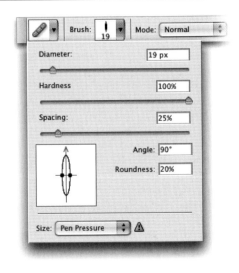

CREATING A CUSTOM SHADOW/HIGHLIGHT DEFAULT

By default, the Shadow/Highlight adjustment command decreases the shadows by 50%, but if you'd prefer to have Shadow/Highlight open flat (with no automatic shadow adjustment), you can set your own defaults. That way, you decide how much, and when, the shadows get opened. You do this by going under the Image menu, under Adjustments, choosing Shadow/Highlight, and then dragging the Shadows Amount slider to 0%. Click on the Show More Options checkbox, and at the bottom of the expanded dialog click on the Save As Defaults button. That's it: Now you get to decide if the shadows get opened up, and how much, because everything's set flat.

GETTING BACK SHADOW/HIGHLIGHT'S FACTORY DEFAULTS

Don't ever be concerned about experimenting in Photoshop CS2's amazing Shadow/Highlight feature—mess with the sliders all you want, because you can always get back to the factory-default settings, even if you've overridden them by saving your own defaults. You do this within the Shadow/Highlight dialog (under Image, under Adjustments) by clicking on the Show More Options checkbox. Then, hold the Shift button, and you'll see the Save As Defaults button at the bottom of the expanded dialog change to the Reset Defaults button. Click it, and the factory defaults are back, baby!

HEALING WITH PRESSURE

If you're using a Wacom tablet and wireless pen with Photoshop, you've probably already uncovered the secret hiding place where Adobe tucked the pressure sensitivity controls. (*Hint:* They're in the Brushes palette.) But if you want to use pressure sensitivity with the Healing Brush, it's in a totally different spot. To turn it on, press Shift-J until you have the Healing Brush tool, then in the Options Bar, click directly on the Brush thumbnail, and a menu will pop up (it's not the standard Brush Picker). At the bottom of the menu, you'll see a Size pop-up menu, where you can choose Pen Pressure.

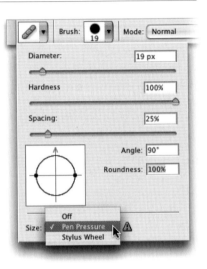

CONTROL THE OPACITY OF YOUR HEALING PROCESS

I don't know if you've noticed, but Photoshop's Healing Brush (Shift-J) doesn't have an option for controlling its opacity (the way the Clone Stamp, Brush, Eraser, and other tools have). But there is a workaround if you want to use the brush and have some control over its opacity. Just go ahead and use the brush first; then to lower the opacity of your

stroke, go under the Edit menu and choose Fade Healing Brush. When the Fade dialog appears, lower the Opacity slider to the desired amount. It's a bit clunky, but it works.

SAY GOOD-BYE TO GRADIENT BANDING

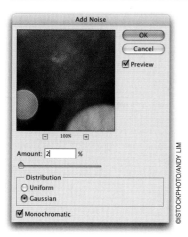

©ISTOCKPHOTO/ANDY LIM

If you've printed an image with a gradient in it, you're probably familiar with banding (a visible line where one color ends and the next starts, like bands of color, instead of a smooth transition from one color to the next). There's a very popular tip for getting rid of banding that's very effective for high-resolution imaging. Open the image in Photoshop and go under the Filter menu, under Noise, and choose Add Noise. When the Add Noise dialog appears, for Amount enter 2, for Distribution choose Gaussian, turn on the Monochromatic checkbox, and then click OK. You'll see a little bit of this noise when viewing the image onscreen, but when printed at high resolution, the noise disappears and hides the banding. We add noise to every gradient we create for just that reason.

SHARPENING YOUR IMAGES LIKE A PRO

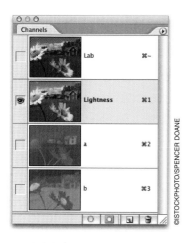

©ISTOCKPHOTO/SPENCER DOANE

Just about every image that is brought into Photoshop, whether from a scanner, digital camera, CD-ROM, etc., needs to be sharpened. The undisputed tool for this task is Photoshop's Unsharp Mask filter. The only downside of using this filter is that getting the level of sharpening you'd like can sometimes cause color shifts and halos, and it can also accentuate dust or specs within the image. There are two ways around this, and what's great about these methods is they let you apply a higher level of sharpening without causing color shifts or other problems: (1) Convert your file from RGB mode to Lab Color. Then go to the Channels palette and click on the Lightness channel. Now apply the Unsharp Mask filter (twice if you need it), then switch back to RGB mode (don't worry, there's no harm in this RGB-to-Lab-to-RGB mode conversion). (2) If you're working on a CMYK image, apply the Unsharp Mask filter, then go under the Edit menu and choose Fade Unsharp Mask. When the Fade dialog appears, change the Mode pop-up menu to Luminosity and click OK (which pretty much does the same thing as method 1; it applies the sharpening to the luminance of the image, not the color).

FIVE TIPS FOR GETTING RID OF MOIRÉ PATTERNS

If you scanned an image that already has been printed in one form or another, you're bound to get a moiré pattern over your image (moiré patterns are a series of dots or spots that appear on your image). These spots are your scanner picking up the halftone screen that was applied when the image was printed.

Here are five quick tips for removing moiré patterns:

1. Go under the Filter menu, under Noise, and choose Despeckle. There are no numbers to input or sliders to adjust—it either works or it doesn't, but luckily, it works about 75% of the time. However, if you run Despeckle and it doesn't work, undo it. That's because Despeckle adds a slight blur to your entire image, and if it doesn't work, there's no sense in leaving that blur applied, eh?
2. Apply a 1-pixel or less Gaussian Blur. This will usually work if method 1 doesn't. Again, if this technique doesn't remove the moiré pattern, undo it to reduce unnecessary blurring.
3. Go under the Filter menu, under Noise, and choose Median. Enter 1 pixel and click OK. I know I'm sounding like a broken record, but if it doesn't work, undo it. You know why.
4. Reduce the resolution of your scan to twice the line screen it will be printed at. For example, if you scanned it at 300 dpi and you're going to print it at 100-line screen, lower the resolution of the file to 200 ppi and that'll probably do the trick. If this image is going to be used on the Web, when you lower the resolution to 72 ppi, that'll probably do it.
5. Lastly, try rescanning the image with the image rotated slightly on the scanner bed. This is a last resort, but if all else fails, this will probably do the trick. Once the image is in Photoshop, you'll have to straighten the scan, but at least the moiré pattern will be gone.

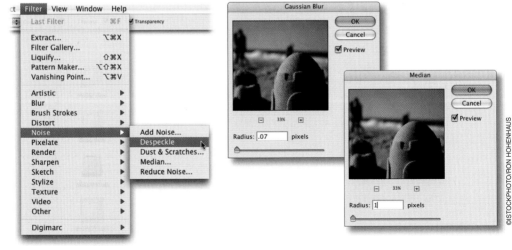

SCAN LINE ART AT THE RESOLUTION YOU NEED

If you're scanning black-and-white line art for reproduction in print, here are two quick tips that'll help you get better results:

1. Scan the line art image at the dpi you'll be printing it. This is the one time we break our long-standing "don't-scan-at-too-high-a-resolution" rule—but only when it comes to line art. If you're going to output your line art on a 600-dpi laser printer, scan it at 600 dpi. If you're going to output it to high-resolution film negs, scan it at 1,200 dpi (that's about as high as you'll need to go).
2. Scan your line art images in Grayscale mode. If you do, then you can apply filters such as the Unsharp Mask to help clean and define the lines, and you can use Levels to brighten the white areas.

Note: If you scan in Bitmap mode, you won't be able to use these two important line art cleanup tips, because they're not supported in Bitmap mode.

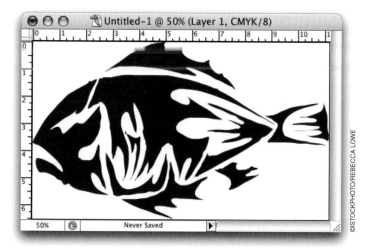

©ISTOCKPHOTO/REBECCA LOWE

USING THE HIGH PASS FILTER FOR SHARPENING

There's a sharpening technique that's really gaining popularity that works especially well on images with lots of well-defined edges (such as buildings, cars, furniture, etc.). It's actually a layer technique combined with a filter, but it's very easy (and often very effective) to apply. Start by duplicating the Background layer of the image you want to sharpen by pressing Command-J (PC: Control-J). Then, go under the Filter menu, under Other, and choose High Pass. When the High Pass dialog appears, enter a Radius of 1.5 pixels (a good starting point) and click OK to apply the filter. It will change your image into a gray mess, but don't sweat it (yet). To bring the sharpening into your image, change the blend mode of this layer to Soft Light. The gray will disappear, and the edges of your image will appear sharper. You can also try the Hard Light mode to increase the sharpening effect. Still not enough? Make a copy of the layer for a multiplying effect. Is one copy not enough sharpening, but two are too much? You can control the sharpening amount in two ways: (1) Switch between Soft Light and Hard Light, or (2) lower the Opacity setting of the layer to dial in just the right amount of sharpening.

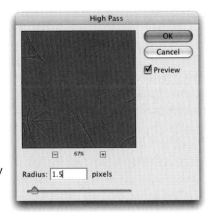

SPOT COLOR GRADIENT FILM SAVER

If you're creating a gradient using a spot color that fades to white, to make sure your gradient appears just on the spot separation plate, create the gradient to go from the spot color to a 0% tint of the same spot color (for example, go from 100% red to 0% red). Just click on the color's opacity stop (that appears above the stop in the color ramp) and then lower the Opacity in the bottom-left corner of the Gradient Editor. That way, when you do your seps, the entire gradient will appear on the red separation.

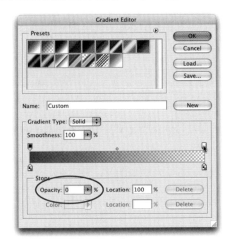

CORRECT IN CMYK OR RGB?

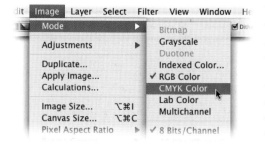

We've been asked the question of whether to correct in CMYK or RGB a hundred times. As a general rule, we try to do as much color correction as possible in RGB mode, and if we're going to use the image on press, we only convert to CMYK at the end of the correction process. The main reason is that CMYK mode throws away data—a lot of data—and why would you want to correct an image with significantly less data than your scanner can capture? We want as much data as possible while correcting images, and when we're done, then we'll convert to CMYK (under Image, choose Mode) and toss the data that won't be used on press.

STRAIGHTENING SCANS IN 10 SECONDS (OR LESS)

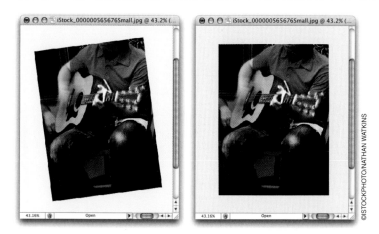

©ISTOCKPHOTO/NATHAN WATKINS

If you've scanned an image and it's crooked when you bring it into Photoshop, you can fix it in about 10 seconds flat. Just switch to the Measure tool (it lives behind the Eyedropper tool in the Toolbox) and drag it along the top edge of the image you want to straighten. That's the hard part (and that should give you an idea of how easy this technique is). Next, go under the Image menu, under Rotate Canvas, and choose Arbitrary. Photoshop automatically enters the amount of rotation (courtesy of your earlier measurement), so all you have to do is click OK and bam!—the image is perfectly straightened.

SCANNERS AREN'T JUST FOR FLAT OBJECTS

Even though your flatbed scanner is normally used for scanning (you guessed it) flat images, it doesn't mean you can't scan images that have more dimension (such as a watch, a ring, a yo-yo, you name it). The only problem is, scanning an image that lifts the lid adds lots of ambient light into your scan, introducing so many outside colors and reflections that it makes the scan all but unusable. The tip for getting around this is deceivingly simple: Just put a black sweater (or black felt cloth) around the object you're going to scan, and you'll get great-looking scans, even with the lid open. The black sweater soaks up that ambient light and you'll be amazed at how natural and balanced your scanned objects will look.

ARE YOUR COLORS PRESS READY?

If you're working on an image that will be printed on a printing press and you select a color that's outside the range of what a CMYK press can reproduce, you'll get what's called a Gamut Warning right within Photoshop's Color Picker. This is just to let you know that the color you've chosen is outside the CMYK gamut. Just below the warning is a tiny color swatch showing you what the color you picked will really look like when printed in CMYK mode. To find out where that color resides within the Color Picker, click once directly on that tiny swatch and Photoshop will pick that color for you.

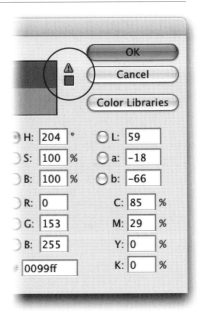

⚫ ⚫ ⚫ NEVER SWAP COLORS AGAIN WHEN CLEANING LINE ART

When cleaning up line art images with the Pencil tool, you can spend a lot of time going back and forth to the Toolbox to switch your Foreground color to black (to fill in missing pixels) and then to white (to erase pixels that shouldn't be there in the first place). It does help if you use the keyboard shortcut D to set your Foreground to black, and then X to make white your Foreground color, but there's actually a faster way. Once you select the Pencil tool, go in the Options Bar and turn on Auto Erase. What the Auto Erase option does is pretty neat—when you click the Pencil in a black area of pixels, it paints white; when you click it on a white pixel, it automatically paints black. It happens automatically—so you never have to switch colors again—saving you a ton of time, travel, and keystrokes.

⚫ ⚫ ⚫ LET PHOTOSHOP DO YOUR RESOLUTION MATH

You don't need a calculator to determine how much resolution you need for printing to a particular line screen—Photoshop will do all the math for you, right inside the Image Size dialog. Here's how: Open the image you want to print. Go under the Image menu and choose Image Size. When the dialog appears, click on the Auto button (it's right under the Cancel button). When the Auto Resolution dialog appears, all you have to do is type in the line screen of the device you're printing to and then choose a Quality setting. Here's how Photoshop does its resolution math:

Draft: This just lowers your resolution to 72 ppi (ideal for onscreen use, the Web, etc.).
Good: This takes the line screen and multiplies it by 1.5.
Best: This doubles the line screen (multiplies it by 2).

When you click OK, Photoshop enters the math it just did into the Resolution field of the Image Size dialog.

GOING TO PRESS? MAKE SURE YOUR MONITOR
IS IN THE "RIGHT SPACE"

By default, the RGB space for your monitor is set to sRGB, which is an okay mode for designing Web graphics. However, if you're producing graphics for print, the sRGB mode is just
about the worst RGB space your monitor could possibly be set at. It clips off lots of colors
that are actually printable in CMYK mode, and therefore is pretty unsuitable for prepress
work. We recommend changing your RGB workspace to an RGB space that's more appropriate for doing print work. We like Adobe RGB (1998), which is a very popular RGB space for
prepress work. You choose this RGB space under the Photoshop menu, under Color Settings
(in Windows, Color Settings can be found under the Edit menu). When the Color Settings
dialog appears, under the Working Spaces area, choose Adobe RGB (1998) from the RGB
pop-up menu.

WANT BETTER GRADIENTS ON PRESS? HERE'S THE TIP

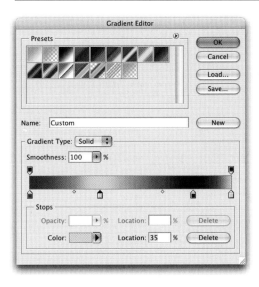

If you're designing a job that will ultimately go to a printing press in CMYK mode and it's going to contain one or more gradients, you'll get better printed results (less color shifts) if you create those gradients after you convert to CMYK mode.

GETTING BEFORE AND AFTER PREVIEWS

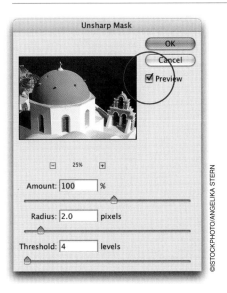

©ISTOCKPHOTO/ANGELIKA STERN

If you're applying a correction filter, such as the Unsharp Mask filter, you can get a before and after view of your image even before you click the OK button (and then press Command-Z [PC: Control-Z] to undo/redo the filter). Instead, click-and-hold on the preview box inside the Unsharp Mask filter. When you click-and-hold, you get the before preview in the window; when you release the mouse button, it shows you how the image will look with the filter applied. Pretty handy. If you need to see the full preview onscreen, you can toggle the Preview checkbox on or off. Another tip is to hold the Command or Option (PC: Control or Alt) button while in a filter dialog, and then your cursor changes into the Zoom tool. You can then zoom in or out in your preview window by clicking within it.

CHAPTER 8 • Image Correction and Prepress Tips   **183**

CLONING FROM IMAGE TO IMAGE

If you're retouching an image using the Clone Stamp tool (S), not only can you clone from the image you're in but you can also clone from any other image that you have open. All you have to do is make sure both images are open at the same time. Go to the other image, Option-click (PC: Alt-click)

on the area you want to clone from, switch back to the image you're working on, and then start painting. When you do, you'll be cloning image data from the other image.

GET MORE REALISTIC DROP SHADOWS ON PRESS

Here's a quick tip for getting more realistic drop shadows in print: Add some noise. When you choose Drop Shadow from the Add a Layer Style pop-up menu in the Layers palette, there's a slider for adding noise

to your shadows in the Layer Style dialog. When you add just a small percentage, it makes your shadows appear more realistic when they show up in print.

MAKING SURE YOUR WHITES ARE REALLY WHITE

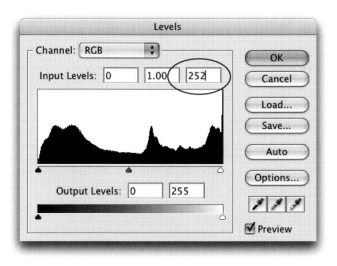

If you have an image that appears to have solid white areas (maybe the background surrounding a logo), but when you put the Eyedropper on that area, it gives you a 1% or 2% reading in one of the CMYK values in your Info palette, you can use Levels to gets those areas back down to 0% so they don't print with a dot. Here's how: Go under the Image menu, under Adjustments, and choose Levels. The third field from the left (at the top of the dialog) shows your current highlight value (your white point setting). The default value will be 255. Enter 252 or 250, then move your cursor over the white area in question and look in the Info palette to see if the readings are now all 0% (that change should be enough to remove the stray colors). When it's right, click OK, and you'll have solid white in your white areas.

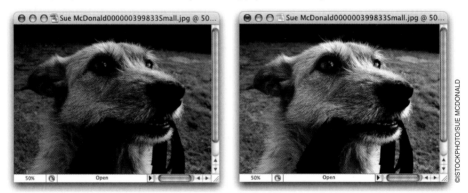

TRY NOT TO CORRECT MORE THAN ONCE

When correcting images in Curves, Levels, etc., it's best to try to do all your corrections at one time rather than changing each setting individually (by that I mean, don't set a highlight in Curves, then close and reopen it to set a shadow). The reason is, each time you apply a tonal correction, it puts some strain on the quality of the image. So to keep your image from having unnecessary data loss, when you open Curves or Levels, make your shadow, highlight, and midtone adjustments, and then click OK to apply all three adjustments at once.

MORE CURVE POINT QUICK TIPS

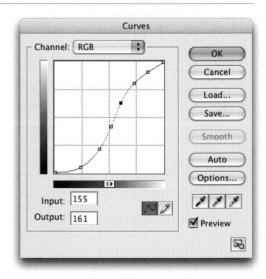

When you're working in Curves (Command-M [PC: Control-M]), once you've plotted a curve point, you can rotate over to the next point in your curve by pressing Control-Tab (PC: Right-click-Tab). To rotate back to the previous point, add the Shift key to make it Shift-Control-Tab (PC: Shift-Right-click-Tab). If you've got one or more points selected and want to deselect all your points, just press Command-D (PC: Control-D) to release all your points.

HAVE PHOTOSHOP HELP FIND YOUR HIGHLIGHTS/SHADOWS

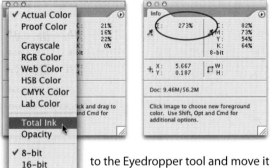

Not sure where the highlight or shadow points in your image are located? Let Photoshop help. Go under the Window menu and choose Info. In the RGB readout, click on the tiny Eyedropper icon to the left of the readout. A pop-up menu will appear with a list of values you can measure. Choose Total Ink from this pop-up menu. Next, press I to switch to the Eyedropper tool and move it over your image in the areas you think might be the darkest. Now, in the Info palette, look for the highest number. When you find the area in your image with the highest number (the highest amount of total ink), you've found the shadow point. Do the same to find the highlight—just look for the lowest number. When you locate that number, you've found the highlight.

TALKIN' 'BOUT MY RESOLUTION

Here's a lingo tip about resolution. Although images can have a resolution from 1 to more than 2,000 ppi, when it comes to talking resolution, there are three basic resolutions that are pretty common. Low-res (short for resolution) is normally 72 ppi, and low-res images are primarily used for onscreen viewing (such as the Web, slide presentations, digital video, etc.). Medium-res is generally 150 ppi and is commonly used for printing to inkjet and laser printers. When people use the term high-res, it's almost always referring to 300 ppi, which is more than sufficient resolution for printing to a printing press. Anything above 300 ppi is still considered high-res, but you'd say it like this: "I made a 600-ppi high-res scan." Which resolution is right for you? Nice try. That's a whole book unto itself.

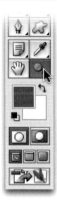

ARE YOU REALLY SEEING YOUR SHARPENING?

When you apply sharpening to your image using the Unsharp Mask or Smart Sharpen filter (under Filter, choose Sharpen), make certain that when you apply it, you're viewing the image at 100% size. Most other views won't give you an accurate view of how the sharpening is really affecting the image. To make sure you're viewing at 100%, just double-click the Zoom tool in the Toolbox.

ADJUSTING CURVE POINTS WITH PRECISION

Once you've plotted a point on a curve in the Curves dialog (Command-M [PC: Control-M]), you can adjust these points by clicking-and-dragging them, but many people find it easier to plot the point by using the Up/Down Arrow keys on their keyboard. This adjusts the Output of the point in increments of 2. To adjust the Input, use the Left/Right Arrow keys. To make larger moves, hold the Shift key while using the Arrow keys and your points will move in increments of 15.

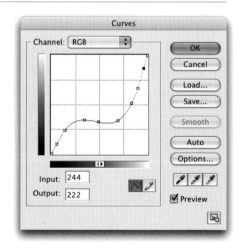

APPLY UNSHARP MASK TO CMYK IMAGES

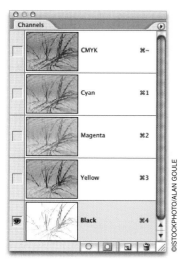

If you've already converted your image to CMYK mode and you want to quickly sharpen your image without introducing color shifts or halos, go to the Channels palette (under the Window menu), click on the Black channel, and apply your Unsharp Mask there. Applying the filter just to the Black channel will enable you to apply a higher level of sharpening without damaging the image.

©ISTOCKPHOTO/ALAN GOULE

RGB FLESH TONES: GETTING THE "RED" OUT

If you're working on an RGB image and you've done your basic color correction but the flesh tone in your image still seems too red (a common problem), here's a tip to fix it fast. First, select the flesh tone areas in your image (using the Lasso tool, etc.). Add a slight feather by going under the Select menu and choosing Feather. Enter a 1-pixel feather for low-res images; 3–5 pixels for high-res images. Go under the Image menu, under Adjustments, and choose Hue/Saturation. From the Edit pop-up menu, choose Reds. Now lower the Saturation slider until your skin tones look more natural and click OK.

ONCE YOU'RE IN CMYK MODE, STAY THERE

You've read some techniques in this chapter that require you to be in either RGB mode or Lab Color mode; however, if for any reason your image is already in CMYK mode, do not (I repeat, do not) convert to RGB or Lab mode for any reason. Once you've converted to CMYK mode, the data loss from the conversion has already occurred, and switching back to RGB mode won't bring back those lost colors. What's worse is, if you switch from CMYK to RGB (or Lab), when you convert back to CMYK mode, you'll go through another CMYK conversion and damage your image even more. The moral of this story is—once you're in CMYK mode, stay there.

THE SIMPLE TIP TO BETTER COLOR SEPARATIONS

Converting from RGB mode to CMYK mode for printing is easy, just choose CMYK from the Mode menu under the Image menu. However, getting great-looking separations on press takes more than just choosing the CMYK menu command. Before you convert to CMYK mode, call the print shop that's printing your job and ask them for their Photoshop CMYK separation setup. They'll provide you with custom settings to input in the Custom CMYK dialog that will give you a separation that's tuned to their particular printing

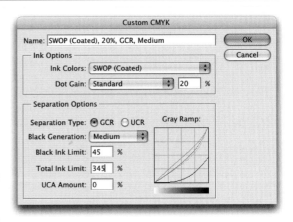

press. Once they provide you with those settings, you input them by going under the Edit menu and choosing Color Settings. When the Color Settings dialog appears, click on the CMYK pop-up menu, and at the top of the menu choose Custom CMYK. The Custom CMYK setup dialog will appear, where you can enter the settings given to you by the print shop. Once entered, then you can make your CMYK conversion, and you'll get a better separation that's specially tuned to the press your job will be printed on.

HOW TO SHARPEN FLESH TONES IN CMYK

©ISTOCKPHOTO/JOEY NELSON

When you're sharpening CMYK images, the toughest areas to sharpen are often the flesh tones. Usually, because of the soft nature of skin, you'll need a lot of sharpening, which can introduce noise and color shifts, particularly in flesh tone areas. One tip that's often used to combat this is to apply your sharpening to just the Cyan channel in the Channels palette in images where flesh tone is the focal point (such as in portraits).

HOW TO READ FOUR AREAS AT ONCE

©ISTOCKPHOTO/CATHERINE SCOTT

Photoshop's Color Sampler tool lets you sample up to four different color readings from within your image at the same time. The cool thing is, anytime you have one of Photoshop's paint tools (Brush, Pencil, etc.), you can instantly access the Color Sampler by holding Option-Shift (PC: Alt-Shift). Click to add a color sampler and the Info palette immediately pops up to show you the reading. Each time you add a sampler, the Info palette expands to show that reading (leaving your earlier readings still visible). To delete any sampler, press Option-Shift (PC: Alt-Shift) again and just move the cursor back over the sampler and it will change into a pair of scissors. Click right on the sampler in your image to delete it. (*Hint:* You have to click directly on the sampler or it won't work, and this doesn't work for all painting tools.)

Before you attempt any of the tips in this chapter, I have to tell you, you'll need a fairly thorough knowledge of calculus, and it wouldn't hurt if you kept a scientific calculator

Speed Kills
advanced tips

handy either. In fact, ideally, you'd put together a team with varied backgrounds and skill sets to really get anything out of this chapter. Believe it or not, that's what some people expect from an "Advanced Tips" chapter—tips that are very complicated and involved. But just because you're a more advanced user, doesn't mean the tips should be harder; it just means the tips apply to more advanced areas of Photoshop use, such as masking, curves, paths, and fun stuff like that. The tips should be easy to do, just covering more advanced topics. But if you really feel you need a complicated and involved tip to get your money's worth, here goes: Open a blank RGB document at 72 ppi. Then take a photograph of your family and tape it to the outside of your monitor. Using the Brush tool, choose a large soft-edged brush, and draw what you see. When complete, it should look exactly like the photograph. Happy now?

ACTION INSURANCE POLICY

Have you ever written an action, and after it's done, you wish you hadn't run it in the first place? Maybe the effect just doesn't look right on the image, or there's a mistake or missing step in your action? Well, here's a tip that will help you, not just when you're testing your action, but even after you've perfected it. Bring up the Actions palette (found under the Window menu), click on the Create New Action icon, and once you're recording, make the first step of your action creating a snapshot. To do this, just open the History palette (under the Window menu) and click on the Create New Snapshot icon at the bottom

of the palette. That way, if after the action runs, you don't like the results, you can just click on the saved snapshot in the History palette, and the image will instantly return to how it looked when you opened it.

DOING ANIMATIONS? DON'T JUMP TO IMAGEREADY

In previous versions of Photoshop, if you wanted to create an animation, you'd have to jump to Image-Ready (Photoshop's Web graphics sibling that comes preinstalled with Photoshop). Although ImageReady still comes with Photoshop CS2, you don't need to jump over there to do your animations; now you can do them right within Photoshop. Just go to the Window menu and choose Animation, and ImageReady's familiar-looking Animation palette will appear across the bottom of your Photoshop screen, and a row of buttons for animation options will appear near the top of your Layers palette.

THE NEW WAY TO CREATE A CLIPPING GROUP

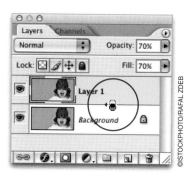

©ISTOCKPHOTO/RAFAL ZDEB

If you're used to the old Command-G (PC: Control-G) shortcut to clip the layer you're on into the layer beneath, then you're going to have some frustrating times in CS2. That's because Command-G (PC: Control-G) now creates a Layer Group, not a clipping group (or clipping mask as Adobe renamed it in CS). To create a clipping mask, you have to use the old shortcut from pre-CS versions of Photoshop, which is to hold the Option key (PC: Alt key) and in the Layers palette click once right between the two layers (your cursor will change to two overlapping circles—that's your cue to click). You unclip them the same way.

KEEPING TRACK OF YOUR EVERY MOVE

If you'd like to keep a running record of every step, every tweak, every movement—virtually every little thing you've done to your image in Photoshop CS2—you can do just that. It's called History Logging. Basically, it keeps a running log (in the background) of all your History States, and it can save it to a text file that you can open and view later. To turn on this History Log, go under the Photoshop menu (PC: Edit menu), under Preferences, and choose General. At the bottom of the Preferences dialog, turn on the checkbox for History Log, then choose if you want the log items embedded into the file (metadata), written to a text file, or both.

EMBED YOUR MESSAGE INTO YOUR PHOTOS

As you know, your digital camera embeds background info into your photos (called EXIF data), and Photoshop embeds its own info when you edit the image (called File Properties). However, in Photoshop CS2 you can add your own info (called IPTC data) in the IPTC Core area within the Metadata palette in Adobe Bridge. This is where you might embed your copyright info, website, or other comments that people viewing your file might find important. To add your info, just click next to any IPTC item that has a Pencil icon to the right of it, and a field will appear where you can enter your own custom info.

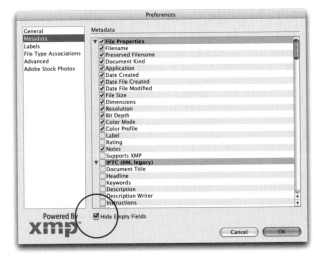

MANAGING THE METADATA OVERLOAD

The Metadata palette in Bridge provides much more information than the average person will ever need. If you don't need all this "metadata overload," you can set it up so it only displays the data you care about, giving you a more orderly, easier-to-read Metadata palette. To do this, go to Bridge's Metadata palette, click on the flyout menu, and choose Preferences. In the dialog that appears, uncheck any fields you don't need displayed, turn on the checkbox at the bottom for Hide Empty Fields, and click OK.

PHOTOSHOP'S OWN SLIDE SHOW

If you don't want to create a full PDF Presentation, you can create a mini slide show right within Photoshop. Just open all the images you want in your slide show, then Shift-click on the Full Screen Mode icon near the bottom of the Toolbox (it's the third icon from the left), and press the Tab key on your keyboard. To step through your slide show, press Control-Tab.

THE HISTOGRAM PALETTE'S VISUAL CUES

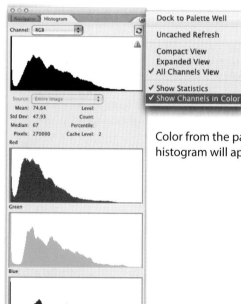

When you're using Photoshop's Histogram palette (under the Window menu), not only can you see a histogram of each individual channel (select the All Channels View option from the Histogram palette's flyout menu), but you can use color as your visual cue to quickly see which channel is which. Just choose Show Channels in Color from the palette's flyout menu, and then the Red channel histogram will appear in red, the Green in green, etc.

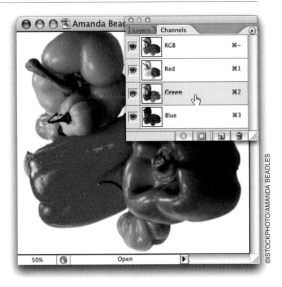

SEEING YOUR FULL-COLOR IMAGE WHILE EDITING A CHANNEL

When you're working on an individual channel in the Channels palette (under the Window menu), by default Photoshop displays your current channel on-screen in grayscale. If you make changes to that channel, you only see how the change affects that channel. However, there is a little-known trick that lets you see the full-color image, while editing the currently selected channel. While you're editing the channel, just press the Tilde key (~), which is right above the Tab key on your keyboard, and you'll see the full RGB preview as you edit.

HOW TO COMBINE TWO PATHS INTO ONE

If you're using the Pen tool (P), and you've created multiple paths within your document, these paths are totally separate, and are moved independently of one another. However, if you want these paths to move as one unit—combine them. Just switch to the Path Selection tool (Shift-A until it comes up), then go up to the Options Bar and click on the Combine button. Now when you move one path, all the combined paths move right along with it.

POWER UP YOUR LAYER STYLES

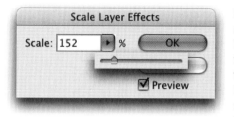

Here's a little-known tip for controlling the intensity of your layer styles. This is particularly helpful if you've applied a number of different layer styles to a layer, and want to affect them all at the same time, rather than tweaking each one individually. It's called Scale Effects, and it's buried in the Layer menu, at the bottom of the Layer Style submenu. Choose it, and a dialog appears with a slider set to 100% by default. As you increase the amount (up to 1000% maximum), it increases the "scale" of all your effects. For example, if you increased the scale of a Drop Shadow layer style, the shadow would become blurrier and its distance from the object would become greater. If you adjusted a Stroke layer style, the stroke would become thicker, etc. Pretty powerful stuff.

FREEFORM/PEN TOOL QUICK SWITCH

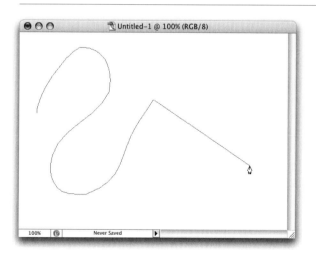

If you're using the Freeform Pen tool (Shift-P until it comes up), there are times when you may want to temporarily switch to the regular Pen tool so you can draw a straight-line segment. You can actually do this by holding the Option key (PC: Alt key) and then releasing the mouse button. This temporarily switches you to the regular Pen tool so you can draw your straight-line segment by moving the mouse. When you're done, click-and-hold, release Option/Alt, and you're back to the Freeform Pen tool.

VISUAL CONTROL OVER YOUR SELECTIONS USING QUICK MASK

Did you know that you can use Quick Mask mode to expand or contract your selections visually? Here's how: Create a selection (using any of Photoshop's selection tools), and then switch to Quick Mask mode (press the letter Q). Now you can go to the Levels dialog (under the Image menu, under Adjustments) and tweak the size of your selection. Moving the midtones Input Levels slider to the far left makes the selected area smaller (contracting the selection). Moving the midtones Input Levels slider to the far right makes the selected area larger (expanding the selection). The changes here usually aren't drastic, so you'd use this technique when a small adjustment to your selection is necessary, but seeing it like this beats the heck out of guessing.

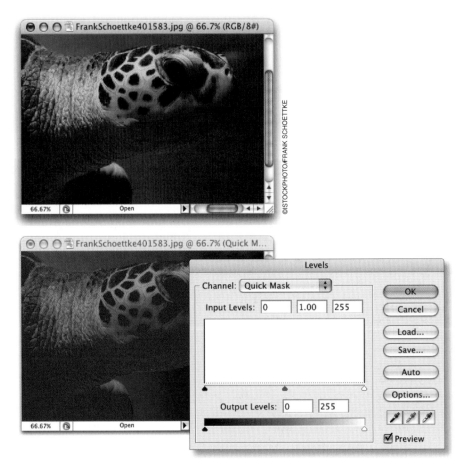

HAVE PHOTOSHOP SELECT THE SHADOWS AND HIGHLIGHTS

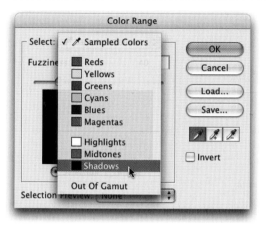

This is a trick we use for prepress and for photo retouching because it instantly lets you select all the shadow areas (or highlight areas if you wish) for a particular image, and it's so easy because Photoshop does all the work. To have Photoshop select just the shadow areas in your image, go under the Select menu and choose Color Range. When the dialog appears, in the Select pop-up menu, choose Shadows (or Highlights), and click OK. The shadow areas are instantly selected. This is ideal for situations where your scanner has plugged up the detail in the shadow areas (pretty common in most sub-$1,000 desktop scanners). Once the shadows are selected, you can "open them up" by going to the Levels dialog (under the Image menu, under Adjustments) and moving the midtones Input Levels slider to the left to bring back some of the shadow detail lost in the scan.

TROUBLESHOOTING ACTIONS? SLOW DOWN!

If you're an advanced user, chances are you're no stranger to using actions, and in fact, you probably create your own (rather than using the default actions that ship with Photoshop, many of which redefine the term "useless"). If you do create your own actions, you've already found that you spend more time troubleshooting your actions than you do creating them in the first place. Well, this little tip makes the troubleshooting process a lot easier, and saves you both time and frustration. The problem is (and this won't sound like a problem) Photoshop runs actions so quickly that you don't see each step, or each dialog, so tracking down a missing or wrong step is just about impossible. Luckily, you can actually slow down your action, or even put a pause between each step, by using Photoshop's Playback Options dialog found in the Actions palette's flyout menu. When it appears, you can choose to play your action Step by Step, seeing everything as it happens, or you can choose to enter the number of seconds you'd like it to pause. Then, when you replay the action, you can see everything step by step and track down the culprit.

ACCESSING GRAYED-OUT FILTERS IN CMYK

One of the bad things about converting from RGB mode to CMYK mode (under the Image menu) is that many of Photoshop's coolest filters can only be applied in RGB mode, and once you're in CMYK mode, many of them are grayed out in the Filter menu, so they can't be accessed. So what do you do if you really want to use one of those filters? (Whatever you do, don't convert back to RGB mode, then back to CMYK. That's image suicide.) Instead, try this tip: In the Channels palette, click on the Cyan channel. Go to the Filters menu and you'll notice that all those grayed-out filters are now suddenly available. All you have to do now is apply the filter you want to each channel individually (once each on Cyan, Magenta, Yellow, and finally the Black channel), and the filter

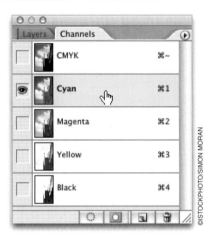

will appear as though you applied it to the entire image (in reality, you did—you just did it the more laborious way). One way to speed up this process is to create an action that will do it all for you with one click of the mouse.

ASSIGNING METADATA TO MULTIPLE FILES

Want to assign metadata to more than one photo at a time in Bridge? (Perhaps you want to embed your copyright info into 30 or more photos at once.) Just Command-click (PC: Control-click) on all the photos you want to affect, then enter the custom info you want (in one of the IPTC fields in the Metadata palette) and that info will be added to every selected photo at once.

⬤ ⬤ ⬤ MORE CONTROL OVER FILTERS

©ISTOCKPHOTO/AMANDA ROHDE

We love Photoshop's Fade command (which acts like an "undo on a slider"), and when it comes to applying filters, we use it all the time to gain more control (including blending mode control) over filters we apply. The only downside to the Fade command (which is found under the Edit menu) is you can only use it one time—you get one opportunity to Fade, or choose a Blend Mode, then you're stuck. Here's a tip to keep the control of your filters for as long as you'd like: When you're about to apply a filter, make a duplicate of the layer before you apply the filter by pressing Command-J (PC: Control-J) and then apply the filter. This keeps the application of your filter fully editable—you can change blend modes as often as you like, change opacity, add a layer mask to determine where the filter shows and where it doesn't, or even toss the layer in the Trash and start over.

APPLYING MULTIPLE FILTERS? NOT ON MY LAYER!

Thinking of applying a number of different filters to a particular layer? Don't do it. Instead, make a copy of your layer by pressing Command-J (PC: Control-J), then apply the first filter. Make another copy of the layer and apply the second filter; make another copy, apply the third filter, and so on. You can use Photoshop's layer blend modes in the Layers palette to get the effect that one filter is applied on top of the others, and now you've got full control over each individual filter applied. If you don't like one of the filters, just drag that layer into the Trash. Better yet, you've got blend and opacity control you wouldn't have by simply applying filter over filter.

NEW SNAPSHOT, THE MISTAKE INSURANCE POLICY

The great thing about Photoshop's History feature is that you can (by default) undo your last 20 steps. Perhaps even more important is that you can always return to how the image looked when you opened it, so you never really do any permanent damage (as long as the file is open). However, what if you opened an image, worked on it for a while, and it was really looking great, but about 10 minutes later, it took a turn for the worse (this happens to us more often than we'd care to admit). If you undo the last 20 steps, it may not take you back far enough to the point that you want to return to, and the only other choice is to go all the way back to where you started. Here's a tip to keep you from pulling your hair out: Any time your image is at a stage where you think it looks pretty good, go to the History palette, and at the bottom of the palette, click on the Create New Snapshot icon. Think of it as an insurance policy, so that if things go bad, you can at least return to that spot and try again. It's not a bad idea to create a new snapshot about every five minutes when you're working on a big project. To keep from loading up on snapshots, when you create a new one, delete one or two snapshots before it.

⬤ ⬤ ⬤ SAVING YOUR ACTIONS AS PRINTABLE TEXT FILES

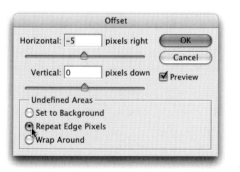

This is a totally undocumented actions tip, and if you need it, it's a real life-saver. Once you've created an action, you can actually save a text document with all the action steps so you can have a printed hard copy of your action. Here's how: In the Actions palette, click on the action set containing the action that you want to save as a text document. Hold Command-Option (PC: Control-Alt) and from the Actions palette's flyout menu, choose Save Actions. When the Save dialog appears, you'll notice that the three-letter file extension is TXT (indicating it's a text file) rather than ATN (which is the Photoshop action format). Click OK and you've got a text file you can open in any word processor to print out your steps.

⬤ ⬤ ⬤ 3D PRINT EFFECTS (AND WHERE TO GET THOSE GOOFY GLASSES)

For a brief time back in the 1950s, 3D movies were all the rage, but it was short-lived, probably because you had to wear those cheesy-looking 3D glasses to experience the effect. Although 3D has come a long way since then, unfortunately you still have to wear the cheesy glasses. Be that as it may, the 3D effect is starting to appear again in print ads in trendy magazines, which generally include the paper 3D glasses in the magazine. This effect can be created in Photoshop, no problem. The hardest part is finding a supplier for 3D glasses (okay, we'll help on that part too. Try 3D Glasses Direct at www.3dglasses.net). Here's a tip on how to create the 3D effect in Photoshop: Open an RGB image, then go to the Channels palette and click on the Red channel. Go under the Filter menu, under Other, and choose Offset. For Horizontal enter –5 and set Vertical to zero. For Undefined Areas, choose Repeat Edge Pixels, then click OK. In the Channels palette, click on the RGB channel to reveal the effect. Then, lastly, you have to determine which part you want to appear as "coming out of the image" toward the person viewing it. Switch to the History Brush (Y), and using a soft-edged brush, paint over the area you want to "jump out" from the image. As you paint with the History Brush, you'll see your original untouched image paint back in (don't sweat it, that's what it's supposed to do). Now all you have to do is order the glasses.

CREATING REUSABLE DIAGONAL GUIDES

If you've used Photoshop's rulers at all, you know that you have your choice of either a vertical or horizontal guide. That's not a bad thing, but there's one thing missing—a diagonal guide. Since Photoshop doesn't have one, here's a tip for making your own: Start by clicking the Create a New Layer icon in the Layers palette, then double-click on your Foreground color swatch and in the resulting Color Picker, set it to R: 161, G: 253, B: 253 (the color Photoshop uses for its built-in guides). Switch to the Line tool found in the Shapes tools (Shift-U until it comes up), and on this new layer draw a diagonal line where you want your guide to appear (make sure you have the Fill Pixels icon selected in the Options Bar). It's not a bad idea to copy that layer into a separate document and save it on your drive—so anytime you need a diagonal line, you can just open that document and drag it right in.

THE SECRETS OF SEARCHING IN BRIDGE

Don't get caught in the trap of thinking that you have to assign keywords to your photos before you can start using Bridge's Find function (although keywords certainly make it easier). But to find out just how much power the Find function really has, just press Command-F (PC: Control-F), then choose your options from the pop-up menus in the Criteria section. If you remember you shot the photo you're looking for with a certain camera, you can search All Metadata for that make and model. You can also search by Rating, Date Created, and a host of other criteria.

DRAG-AND-DROP CURVES FOR QUICK CORRECTION

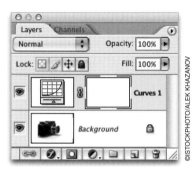

If you're color-correcting a number of images that are basically the same (for example, catalog shots or high school yearbook shots, where the lighting and composition are pretty much the same), you may want to apply the same Curve setting to a number of images. Rather than saving the Curve setting and loading it each time, try this tip: Use the Create New Adjustment Layer pop-up menu at the bottom of the Layers palette to create a Curves adjustment layer, and then just drag-and-drop that adjustment layer from your current image to your target image.

©ISTOCKPHOTO/ALEK KHAZANOV

ACTIONS POWER TIP: ADD AN ACTION TO YOUR ACTION

Here's an actions power tip: Did you know that you can build an action that will include an existing action? Here's how it's done: As you're recording your action, just go to the Actions palette, click on the existing action you want to include in your current action, and click the Play button at the bottom of the Actions palette. The existing action will now be added as a step in your current action (pretty scary stuff).

⚫ ⚫ ⚫ PREPRESS CLEANUPS—IN A SNAP

This is a great tip if you're zoomed in close to an image for retouching, or checking it in prepress for spots or specs, because it lets you check the entire image in a very methodical way—using your keyboard to navigate zone by zone. Here's how:

Press the Home key to jump to the upper-left corner of your image window.
Press the End key to jump to the lower-right corner of your image window.
Press the Page Up key to scroll upward one full screen.
Press the Page Down key to scroll downward one full screen.
Press Command-Page Up (PC: Control-Page Up) to scroll one full screen to the left.
Press Command-Page Down (PC: Control-Page Down) to scroll one full screen to the right.

Once you've learned these shortcuts, you can start by pressing the Home key (jumping you to the upper left-hand corner of your image). Clean that area then press the Page Down key to move methodically down the left side of your image until you reach the bottom of your window. Then press Command-Page Up (PC: Control-Page Down) to move one screen to the right, clean that area, then press the Page Up key to move methodically up the image until you reach the top. Repeat these steps until you're finished. The advantage of doing it this way, besides the sheer speed of using keyboard shortcuts, is that you'll see every area of the image without missing a spot.

⚫ ⚫ ⚫ NO MORE CREATING TYPE IN CHANNELS

If you've ever tried to create and format type in a channel, you know what a pain it can be. Especially because, when you're working in a channel, it doesn't create an editable Type layer, so you're really limited to how you can format and, of course, edit your type. So instead of creating type in a channel (which many special channel-type effects call for), just create your type on a layer as usual. In fact, don't go to the Channels palette at all—just pretend you're not using channels. Once you've got your type formatted and adjusted just the way you want

it on your regular Type layer, Command-click (PC: Control-click) on your Type layer's thumbnail in the Layers palette. This puts a selection around your type. Now you can go under the Select menu and choose Save Selection. When the dialog appears, click OK, and it saves your perfectly formatted type as (you guessed it) a channel. Now you can delete your Type layer, and you're left with an Alpha channel with perfectly formatted type.

BLEND MODE POWER TIP

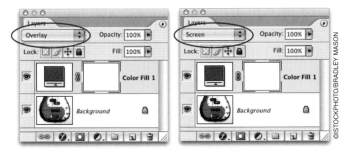

Once you understand layer blend modes, you wind up using them all the time. Chances are by now you know which individual modes you want to use (such as Overlay, Multiply, Soft Light, Hard Light, Screen) and which ones you'll probably never use (such as Dissolve). If you know which ones you want to apply, you can use a keyboard shortcut to jump right to the blend mode you want. For example, to jump to the Overlay mode for a layer, press Option-Shift (PC: Alt-Shift) and the first letter of the mode you want, in this case, the letter O (making the shortcut Option-Shift-O [PC: Alt-Shift-O]). For Screen mode, you'd press Option-Shift-S (PC: Alt-Shift-S), and so on. (*Note:* If you have a tool selected that has a blend mode in its Options Bar, such as the Brush tool [B], the keyboard shortcut will change that tool's blend mode instead of the layer blend mode.)

LET PHOTOSHOP TELL YOU THE HIGHLIGHT AND SHADOW

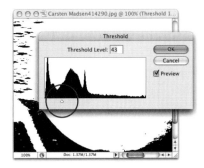

We use this tip to have Photoshop help us determine which are the darkest (shadow) points and which are the lightest (highlight) points in an image when we're color-correcting. We start by choosing a Threshold adjustment layer from the Create New Adjustment Layer pop-up menu at the bottom of the Layers palette. When the Threshold dialog appears, we drag the slider all the way to the left and the image turns completely white. We then slowly drag the slider back to the right, and the first black pixels that appear onscreen are the shadow areas. We make a mental note of that area as our shadow point. Then we drag the slider all the way to the far right (the image turns black). As we drag slowly back toward the left, the first white pixels that appear are the highlight points in the image. We note them as well. We now know where the shadow and highlight points are in the image, and we can use them, along with the Eyedropper tools in the Curves dialog (Command-M [PC: Control M]), to set the proper shadow and highlight areas to remove any color casts. *Note:* When you've determined where the shadow and highlight areas are, you can then delete the Threshold adjustment layer by dragging it into the Trash icon at the bottom of the Layers palette.

USING THE LASSO—DON'T STOP TO NAVIGATE

If you're using the Lasso tool (L), you have a surprising amount of navigation control, even while you're dragging out your selection. For example, if you're drawing a selection and you need to scroll over a bit, just press-and-hold the Spacebar, and right where your cursor is, the Hand tool will appear. Then you can move the image while you're still selecting (try it once and you'll see what we mean). When you let go of the Spacebar, you're right where you left off, and you can continue your selection. Here's another Lasso tip: If you're drawing a selection and reach the edge of your document window and need to scroll over, hold the Option key (PC: Alt key), let go of the mouse button, move your mouse to the edge of your image window, and you can nudge the screen over (again, this is one you have to try once to understand it). It's like you're using the Lasso tool to slide the image over. When you're done sliding, press the mouse button and release Option/Alt to continue selecting. Incidentally, while selecting, you can also use the zoom in/out tricks: Command–+ (Plus Sign) (PC: Control–+) and Command–– (Minus Sign) (PC: Control––).

LOAD ANY SAVED SELECTION WITHOUT THE CHANNELS PALETTE

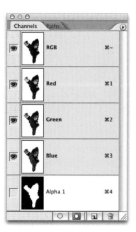

If you're working on an RGB image and you've saved a selection (by drawing a selection and choosing Save Selection from the Select menu), you can instantly reload that selection at any time, without going to the Channels palette. If you have only one saved selection, just press Command-Option-4 (PC: Control-Alt-4), and the selection will instantly appear onscreen. If you have a second saved selection, press Command-Option-5 (PC: Control-Alt-5), and so on. The key to remember is that the RGB channels take up the 1, 2, and 3 spots, so always start with 4 to load your first Alpha channel. *Note:* If you're working with CMYK images, remember to always start with 5, because the CMYK channels take up the first four spots.

PLOT MULTIPLE CURVE POINTS IN JUST ONE CLICK

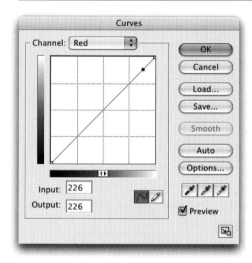

Earlier in the book, we showed you how Photoshop will plot a point on the curve for you if you Command-click (PC: Control-click) on a color in your image that you want plotted. However, there's a power tip that we waited until now to share—if you add the Shift key, making it Command-Shift-click (PC: Control-Shift-click), Photoshop will add a point for that spot on all the color channels for you. This works in both RGB and CMYK modes.

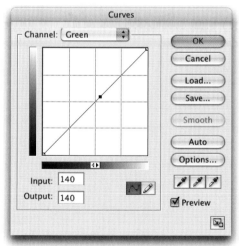

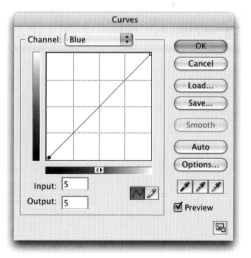

TOUGH SELECTION TIP

If you're struggling to make a selection of an image that's against either a background of a similar color or a very busy background, here's a masking tip to make the process easier: Add a Levels or Curves adjustment layer above your image layer using the Create New Adjustment Layer pop-up menu, and use it to dramatically increase the contrast in the image to help make the edges stand out. This will often help make the difference between the object's edge and the background more obvious. The great part is, you can totally damage the look of the image because you're using an adjustment layer. When your selection is in place, just drag the adjustment layer onto the Trash to delete it, and your image is back to normal, but you've got that "impossible" selection still in place.

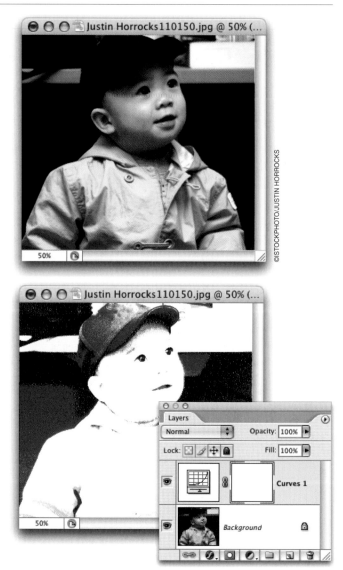

MAKING THE COLOR PICKER SHOW CMYK

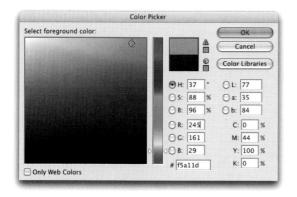

If you're working in CMYK mode and you go to the Color Picker, it still displays RGB colors. This is a bit of a problem, because you think you're picking one color, but when you start to paint or fill with that color, you get the CMYK desaturated version. Here's a tip to get around that. When you're in CMYK mode and you go to the Color Picker, press Command-Y (PC: Control-Y), which is the shortcut for Proof Colors (found under the View menu). When you do this with the Color Picker open, it changes all the colors in the Color Picker to CMYK colors. That way, when you pick a color in the Color Picker, it looks the same when you paint or fill with it in your CMYK image.

MOVING MULTIPLE CURVE POINTS AT ONCE

If you're working in the Curves dialog (Command-M [PC: Control-M]) and you want to make more than one point active at the same time, click on one point (to make it active) then hold the Shift key and click on another. As long as the Shift key is held down, you can click on as many points as you'd like to make them active at the same time.

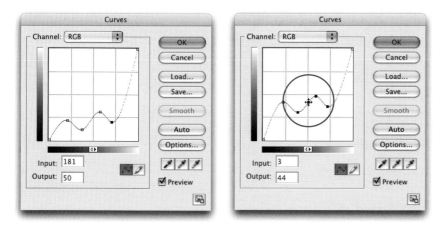

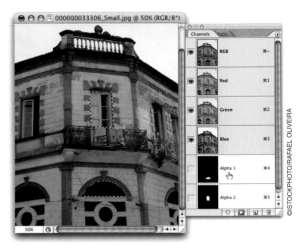

● ● ● ADD TO YOUR SELECTIONS THROUGH THE CHANNELS PALETTE

If you've got the Channels palette open and you have multiple saved Alpha channels, you can load any Alpha channel as a selection by holding the Command key (PC: Control key) and clicking directly on the channel's name. This instantly loads the selection. An even better tip: If you hold the Command key (PC: Control key) then add the Shift key (making it Command-Shift/Control-Shift) and click on another Alpha channel, it adds that to your current selection. You can keep adding more selections to your original selection until, well… until you run out of Alpha channels.

● ● ● EMBEDDING PATHS INTO ACTIONS

If you're creating actions and you want your action to include a path that you've created, you can do that, but you have to draw your path first, before you record your action. Once you've drawn your path, and it comes to the part of your action that requires the path, go to the Action palette's flyout menu, choose Insert Path, and that path will be stored along with the action.

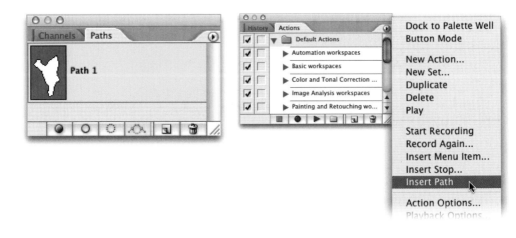

MEASURE TWICE, LOOK ONCE

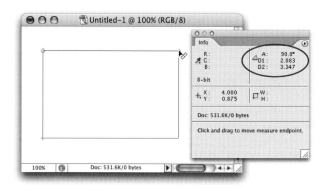

If you need to measure more than one side of an object (for example, if you're measuring a box, and you need the height and width), you can measure both at the same time. First, open the Info palette under the Window menu (so you can see the measurements that the Measure tool generates), then get the Measure tool (Shift-I until it comes up) and click-and-drag it along the first edge. Release the mouse when you reach the end of the edge. Then hold the Option key (PC: Alt key), click on the end of the first line, and continue on in a different direction. You'll notice that another measurement line appears. Now, look in the Info palette and you'll see your two measurements listed under D1 and D2.

STROKING HALF A PATH—HALF A PATH????

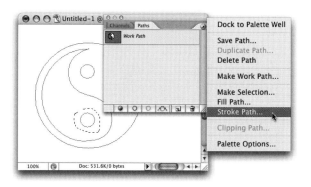

This is a mind-blowing advanced tip (not because it's hard—it's simple—but if you use the Pen tool [P], warning—your mind is about to spontaneously combust). Here's the scoop: If you're an advanced user, you already know that you can draw a path and then apply a stroke along that path (using the paint tool of your choice) by choosing Stroke Path from the Paths palette's flyout menu. But dig this: If you draw your path, but only want to stroke a portion of that path, all you have to do is make a selection (using any selection tool) of the part of the path you want stroked. Then when you choose Stroke Path, it will only stroke the area of your path that is contained within your selection. Boom! That was the sound of our heads exploding.

⬤ ⬤ ⬤ LOCKING A PDF PRESENTATION

If you're using Photoshop to create a PDF Presentation slide show (under the Automate submenu in the File menu) so you can email it to your clients for proofing, one of your concerns may be that your client will just print your photos out to a photo-quality printer, leaving you out in the cold (so to speak). But you can pull the plug on their printing aspirations. When saving your PDF Presentation, under Output Options, choose Presentation, then hit Save. It'll ask you to name your PDF presentation (you're not done yet), so name it and click Save. Then, a PDF options dialog will appear. Under Security (in the options along the left side), turn on the checkbox for Use a Password to Restrict Printing, Editing and Other Tasks under Permissions. Enter (and memorize) a password. Then, make sure Printing Allowed and Changes Allowed are set to None. Click Save PDF and it'll ask for your password one more time. Now, when you email the PDF Presentation, printing will be grayed out, and even if they have the full version of Acrobat, they won't be able to copy-and-paste your photos into something else for printing.

Save Adobe PDF

Adobe PDF Preset: [High Quality Print]

Standard: None Compatibility: Acrobat 5 (PDF 1.4)

General
Compression
Output
Security
Summary

Security

Encryption Level: High (128–bit RC4) – Compatible with Acrobat 5 and Later

Document Open Password
☐ Require a password to open the document

Document Open Password: [   ]

Permissions
☑ Use a password to restrict printing, editing and other tasks

Permissions Password: [********]

ⓘ This password is required to open the document in PDF editing applications.

Printing Allowed: None

Changes Allowed: None

☐ Enable copying of text, images and other content
☐ Enable text access of screen reader devices for the visually impaired
☐ Enable plaintext metadata

(Save Preset...) (Cancel) (Save PDF)

SPEEDING UP BATCH ACTIONS

If you're running a Batch action on a folder full of images, one of the things that can really slow the process down is the fact that the History palette keeps creating History States (undos) for each image. To keep your Batch actions running at full speed, there are two things you can do: In the History palette's flyout menu, under History Options, turn off the checkbox for Automatically Create First Snapshot. Secondly, go under the Photoshop menu, under Preferences, and choose General (in Windows, Preferences can be found under the Edit menu). In the History States field, lower the number from 20 (the default) to 2 and click OK, then your Batch will run like a greased pig. Don't forget to increase your History States or change your History Options back after you're done batching or you'll be down to two undos.

PUTTING YOUR LENS FLARE ON THE SPOT

This tip lets you precisely position the center of the Lens Flare filter by using the Info palette and a little-known feature of the Lens Flare dialog. First, open the Info palette (found under the Window menu), then put your cursor over the precise spot in your image where you'd like the center of your lens flare to appear. Look in the Info palette, under the X and Y coordinates, and write down those two coordinates (I knew one day I'd find a use for the X and Y coordinate readings). Then go under the Filter menu, under Render, and choose Lens Flare. There's a fairly large preview window in the center of the dialog. Hold the Option key (PC: Alt key), click once on the preview window, and it brings up the Precise Flare Center dialog. Enter those X and Y coordinates you wrote down earlier (you did write them down, right?), click OK, and your lens flare is precisely positioned.

I've got to be honest with you, I'm not sure you really need this chapter, so let's do a little quiz to start things off, and if for some reason you fail this impromptu quiz, then you'll have to

Fast Company
troubleshooting tips

read the chapter. Pass, and you jump straight to Chapter 11. Ready? Begin (you have 12 minutes for the first segment). Question One: If Photoshop crashes while copying a 50-MB file into Clipboard memory, do you (a) pack up your computer, call Billie Joe MacAllister, and ask him to meet you at the Tallahatchie bridge; (b) completely disrobe, sit cross-legged on the floor while burning candles around the Photoshop product box; (c) press Shift-Alt-Control-Delete-Tilde-Tab-Escape-Enter-Option-F15-Backslash, proving you have 11 fingers; or (d) all of the above? Answer: It was a trick question. Obviously, the real answer would have been "b," except you never, never dare to have an open flame anywhere near your Photoshop product box. Sorry, grasshopper—turn the page and start reading.

THE REAPPEARING/DISAPPEARING BRUSH TIP

This one gets more people because it's a feature that acts like a bug. Has this ever happened to you? You're working in Photoshop, you're using the Brush tool (B), and everything seems fine. But a little later in your session, you get the Brush tool again, and it no longer displays the size of the currently selected brush tip. Instead, it displays a little crosshair cursor. So you go to the Preferences dialog and choose Display & Cursors, and sure enough, you've got Normal Brush Tip chosen as your preference, but for some strange reason, it's not showing your brush size; it's showing that stupid crosshair. Here's the problem: Check your Caps Lock key. It's turned on, and turning it on changes your Brush cursor from displaying brush size to displaying the crosshair. This is actually a feature to be used when you need to see the precise center of your brush. The problem is it's assigned to the Caps Lock key, so every time you turn on Caps Lock when you're working with type, you just temporarily switched your Brush cursor (or any cursor for that matter). Does Adobe need to find a better key for this feature/bug? You betcha! Will it happen? Not as far as I know.

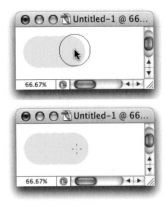

GET PRINT RESOLUTION FROM YOUR DIGITAL CAMERA IMAGES

Problem: You imported an image from your digital camera and although the physical dimensions of the image are rather large, the resolution shows up as only 72 ppi. How can you get enough resolution to print this image? Solution: Go under the Image menu and choose Image Size. Turn off Resample Image, then in the Resolution field, type the resolution you need for the specific device you'll be printing to. When you do this, Photoshop will automatically input the Height and Width that would result from using that resolution (the image size will definitely be smaller—the higher the resolution needed, the smaller the physical dimensions of your image). All you have to do is click OK and Photoshop will do the math, creating an image in the new smaller size, with the new higher resolution. The good news is that by doing it this way, there's absolutely no loss of quality to the file whatsoever.

HOW TO USE RGB FILTERS ON GRAYSCALE IMAGES

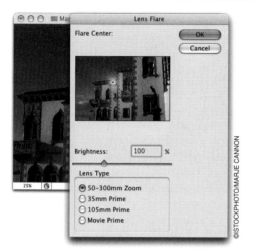

If you're working on grayscale images, you'll find there are some Photoshop filters that won't work (they're grayed out, so you can't access them). Of course, it's always the really cool filters, such as Lens Flare and Lighting Effects, that are grayed out. But don't be dismayed (in fact, be "mayed") because you can still use those filters—just switch to RGB mode (it's found under the Image menu, under Mode), apply the filters, then switch back to Grayscale mode. It won't affect the color of your image because, well, there is no color—you're working on a grayscale image. Switching to RGB doesn't suddenly pour color onto your image; your grayscale image will still look grayscale in RGB. When you switch back to Grayscale mode (after applying the filters), you'll get a warning asking, "Discard color information?" You can safely click OK, because after all, there was no color to begin with.

STOP THE CROP SNAPPING

Problem: When you're trying to crop an image using the Crop tool (C), your cropping border tries to snap to the edges of your document window. This might be happening when drawing large Marquee selections as well. Solution: Press Command-Shift-; (PC: Control-Shift-;), which is the shortcut for turning off this snapping. The only downside is it turns off all snapping (like Snap To Guides, Snap To Grid, etc.). If you just want the Crop snapping (or Marquee snapping) off, go under the View menu, under Snap To, and choose Document Bounds, and your tools will no longer try to snap to your, well, document bounds.

LET'S DO THE TEXT WARP AGAIN

I get more people than you can "stick a shake at" asking me about this problem. If you go to use Photoshop's Warped Text function, you might get a warning that states, "Could not complete your request because the type layer uses a faux bold style." A faux

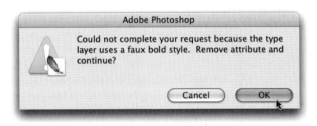

bold style? What in the wide world of sports is that? Actually, it's a feature of Photoshop (that was introduced back in version 5.0) that lets you create a fake (faux) bold or italic type style for fonts that don't really have a bold or italic type style. It's toggled on/off in the Character palette's flyout menu. In Photoshop 7.0, Adobe added the option in the warning dialog to "Remove attribute and continue." All you have to do is click OK to remove the faux bold and now you can warp your text. Life is good.

UNLOCKING THE BACKGROUND LAYER

Can't move the Background layer? That's because back in Photoshop 6.0, Adobe locked the Background layer from movement. That wouldn't be so bad, except that if you look at the top of the Layers palette, you can see that "Yup, the checkbox to lock movement is turned on," but the frustrating part is that it's also grayed out, so you can't simply uncheck it to unlock it. The only way around this is to double-click on the Background, which brings up the New Layer dialog. Click OK, and your Background layer becomes Layer 0 and is unlocked. Now you can move it.

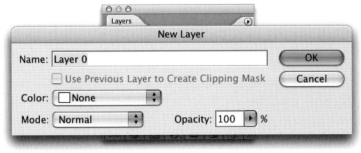

⬤ ⬤ ⬤ DO YOU HAVE ENOUGH RAM? ASK PHOTOSHOP

Not sure if you have enough RAM? Just ask Photoshop. Believe it or not, it can tell you. Here's how: Open a document that's indicative of the type of image you normally work on. Work on the image, doing typical stuff, for about 10 minutes. Along the bottom left-hand corner of your document window, just to the right of the current document magnification readout, is the status bar. By default, it's set to display your document's file size, but if you click-and-hold on the right-facing triangle to the right of it, a pop-up menu of options will appear. Choose Show, then Efficiency. If the percentage shown is 100%, you're gold, baby! That means that Photoshop is running at peak efficiency, because 100% of the time your image manipulations are being handled in RAM. If the efficiency number shown is, say, 75%, this means that 25% of the time, Photoshop ran out of RAM and had to use free hard drive space to make up for it, which means Photoshop ran much slower 25% of the time. An efficiency of 75% is pretty much as low as you want it to go. If it shows anything less than 75%, it's time to buy more RAM. Pronto!

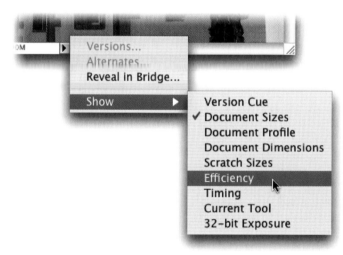

GETTING BETTER EPS PREVIEWS

Problem: The image looked great in Photoshop, but now that you've converted it to
CMYK, saved the file as a TIFF, and placed it
into QuarkXPress, InDesign, PageMaker, etc.,
the image looks awful—way oversaturated
and totally whacked. Reason: The preview
of CMYK TIFFs just looks like that, so don't
freak out—if it looked right in Photoshop,
it should print fine. Okay, what if you saved
the file as an EPS, and when you place the
image into your page-layout app, the color
of the image looks okay, but it's not crisp
and clear, but pixelated. Reason: By default,

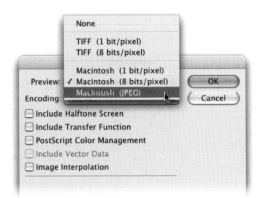

the preview embedded within EPS images is a lame 256-color preview. Solution: When you
choose Save As (from the File menu), choose Photoshop EPS in the Format pop-up menu,
click Save, and the EPS Options dialog will appear. In the Preview pop-up menu, choose
JPEG. That way, it sends a 24-bit, full-color preview, rather than the lame 256-color preview.

GET BACK YOUR BACKGROUND LAYER

Lost your Background layer? It
happens. It's heartbreaking, but
it happens. If you suddenly find
yourself staring at a Layers palette
and there's no Background layer
(chances are you accidentally converted your Background layer into
a regular layer), here's how to get
a Background layer again: Click on
the Create a New Layer icon, then
go under the Layer menu, under
New, and choose Background
From Layer, and Photoshop will

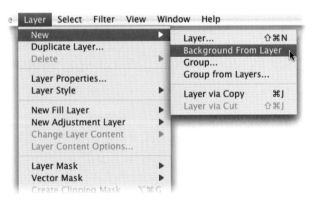

take your new blank layer and create a solid white Background layer at the bottom of your
layer stack.

⬤ ⬤ ⬤ EXPANDING RECTANGULAR SELECTIONS

If you've ever tried to expand a rectangular selection by more than five or six pixels, you know what happens. The crisp, sharp-edged corners that you start off with become rounded. Here's the fix: Don't use the Expand command (found under the Select menu, under Modify). First, make your selection and press Command-T (PC: Control-T) to bring up the Free Transform bounding box. Go to the Options Bar and Control-click (PC: Right-click) in the Width and Height fields to change the measurements from Percent to Pixels. Now, simply add the amount of pixels you want to expand to the existing number. For example: If the field reads 110 pixels, and you want to expand it by 10 pixels, enter 120 pixels in the field and press Enter to apply the transformation. Don't forget to change both the Width and Height fields. That's it—perfectly expanded corners.

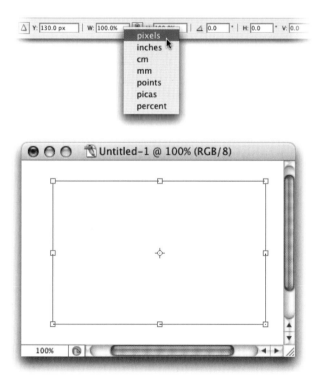

● ● ● FIXING THE "ROUNDED CORNERS" SELECTION PROBLEM

Ever have this happen? You draw a selection with the Rectangular Marquee tool (M) and the corners of your selection are rounded, rather than nice and straight? This happens to a lot of people, especially if they've been drinking. If you haven't been drinking but you're suffering from rounded-corner selections, look up in the Options Bar, and you'll see a field for Feather. Chances are there's some number other than zero in this field, and what's happening is every time you draw a selection with that tool, it's automatically feathering (softening) the edge. What probably happened is you intentionally (or accidentally) added a feather amount at some time, then later forgot to set it back to its default of zero. So to fix it, just highlight the field and type 0 (zero). Incidentally, this is a great Photoshop prank to play on co-workers, friends, soon-to-be-enemies, etc., because the Feather field is usually the last place they'll look.

● ● ● MAKING GLOBAL LIGHT WORK FOR YOU

Problem: You applied a drop shadow to an object on one layer, then later you applied a bevel on another layer, but in the Bevel and Emboss options in the Layer Style dialog, you notice that the position of your drop shadow just moved when you changed the angle of your bevel. Reason: Adobe uses a feature (that acts like a bug) called Global Light. The idea behind it makes sense, yet we've never run into the scenario it was created for. The idea is this: You've created an image with lots of drop shadows, all casting in a particular direction. If the client saw your work and said, "Hey, instead of having the shadows go down

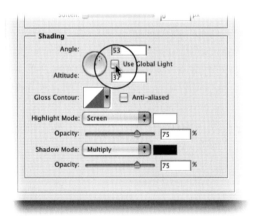

and to the right, can we make all the shadows go up and to the left?" If that unlikely event ever occurred, you'd be set, because all you'd have to do is move one shadow and all the other shadows on other layers would move to the exact same angle. It's a great idea; it just never happens (okay, it's probably happened somewhere, once). Solution: In the Layer Style dialog, deselect the Use Global Light checkbox. Now you can move the angle of your current layer style separately from the rest of your image. Life is good once more.

FIND THE HIDDEN MAGNETIC PEN TOOL OPTIONS

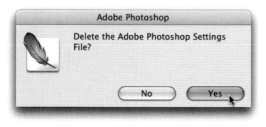

I know what you're thinking—finding the Magnetic Pen tool options? I didn't even know there was a Magnetic Pen tool in the first place. Adobe has done a great job of hiding it. For some reason they must hate this tool. Anyway, to get to the Magnetic Pen tool (the magnetic part means it snaps to well-defined edges to help you draw accurate paths around objects), you have to start by choosing the Freeform Pen tool from the Toolbox (it's nested with the Pen tool). Only then will the subterranean Magnetic checkbox surface in the Options Bar. However, to access the all-important Magnetic options so you have a chance in hell of actually controlling this tool, you have to dig deeper into the underground world of CS2 to make these options bubble to the top. Click on the down-facing black triangle to the right of the Custom Shape tool icon in the Options Bar to reveal a pop-down menu few will ever see—the Freeform Pen Options. In this rarely viewed menu, you'll find a checkbox for Magnetic, and clicking on it will bring the grayed-out Magnetic options to life, and open a treasure chest of newfound riches (also known as more boring options).

LET PHOTOSHOP REBUILD YOUR PREFS

If you need to delete Photoshop's current preferences file (which is a common "first-line-of-defense" troubleshooting move), you don't have to go digging around your drive. All you have to do is hold the Command, Option, and Shift keys (PC: Control-Alt-Shift) when you first launch Photoshop, and you'll be greeted with a dialog asking you if you want to delete the Photoshop Settings File. If you do, click Yes, and Photoshop will build a new, factory-fresh set of preferences for you.

STOP THE "CLICK-AND-JUMP-TO-THAT-LAYER" BLUES

Problem: All of a sudden, every time you click on a layer with the Move tool, it jumps to that layer. Solution: Somehow you turned on a feature called Auto Select Layer, which lets you make a layer active by just clicking on it with the Move tool. To turn this feature off, press V to get the Move tool, and up in the Options Bar, turn off the checkbox for Auto Select Layer. Besides, you never really need to turn this feature on, because you can just hold the Command key (PC: Control key) and click on any layer in your image window.

FASTER APPLICATION SWITCHING

Do you often copy-and-paste images from Photoshop into other applications (such as FileMaker Pro, Word, etc.)? I'm not talking about importing a TIFF or EPS, I'm talking about copying the object, switching to another application, and pasting your copied image from the Clipboard. You don't? Great, then we have a tip for you that will speed up your application-switching pretty dramatically. Go under the Photoshop menu, under Preferences, under General, and turn off the checkbox for Export Clipboard (in Windows, Preferences can be found under the Edit menu). Here's what's happening when it's turned on: Whatever you last copied in Photoshop gets transferred to your system's Clipboard memory when you switch to another application, just in case you want to paste it. If you have a large image in Clipboard, it'll take some time to export the image to the other application (or it'll be so large it won't export at all—you'll get a warning dialog instead). So, turn off that preference, and wait no more.

WILL MORE RAM MAKE PHOTOSHOP RUN FASTER?

Problem: You added more RAM to your system and assigned more RAM to Photoshop, but it doesn't seem to run any faster. Reason: Adding RAM doesn't always make Photoshop run faster. It only works if you didn't have enough RAM to begin with. Adding RAM will only help to make your computer run as fast as it can, but it won't make your 800-MHz computer run at 801 MHz. For example, if you work on Web images and the average image you work on is 3 MB, you only need about 15 or 20 MB assigned to Photoshop to have it run at full speed. If you've got that, and add another 256 MB of RAM, Photoshop won't run any faster, because Photoshop only needs that 15 or 20 MB that you already had. Freaky. To check your RAM usage, go under the Photoshop menu, under Preferences, and choose Memory & Image Cache (on a Windows PC, Preferences are under the Edit menu).

DON'T USE CROP TO FIX BARREL DISTORTION

©ISTOCKPHOTO/BRUCE LIVINGSTONE

Problem: You're trying to fix barrel distortion that appears on a photo you're editing, but using the Crop tool's Perspective feature is a guessing game. You try the crop and it doesn't look right; you have to undo it, and guess again. Solution: Don't use the Crop tool's Perspective feature (found in the Options Bar), even though it was specifically de-signed to address barrel distortion. Use the stan-dard Free Transform command instead by pressing Command-T (PC: Control-T) and then pressing-and-holding the Command (PC: Control) key while you drag the corner handles to create your perspective. Doing this gives you a live onscreen preview as you work, so fixing the distortion takes just a few seconds—unlike Crop's Perspective.

⬤ ⬤ ⬤ GETTING SMALLER PHOTOSHOP FILES

Do your Photoshop PSD file sizes seem a little large? It may be because of a Preferences setting that makes Photoshop save a flattened version of your Photoshop image, along with your layered Photoshop file. Why does Photoshop do this? Because there's a slight possibility you might share this file with someone using Photoshop 2.5 (just like there's a slight possibility that Congress will vote to cut their own salaries), and Photoshop 2.5 didn't support layers, so it can't read your layered document. But because, by default, that flattened version is included in your layered file, guess what—2.5 can open the flattened image. What luck! Who cares? I'd rather have smaller file sizes all year long, and if you would too, go under the Photoshop menu (the Edit menu in Windows), under Preferences, under File Handling, then in the File Compatibility section, for Maximize PSD and PSB File Compatibility, change Ask to Never. Think about this one for a minute and you'll wonder why this is turned on by default. Think about it for two minutes and you'll wonder why it's in Photoshop at all. Don't spend too much time on it, or you'll start to wonder who's the poor soul that's stuck on version 2.5.

The reason I call this chapter "Killer Web Tips" is that most of the tips in this chapter came from a buddy of mine who's now serving time in Raiford State Penitentiary for

Speed Freak
killer web tips

manslaughter. Technically, he's not really a killer, and technically this chapter should have been called "Web Tips from a Killer" rather than "Killer Web Tips," but really, would you have bought this book if that was the name of this chapter? You would have? Wow! You're my kind of person (or trusty, as my friend likes to call them). Seriously though, in this chapter we're going to look at some tips to make optimizing your graphics easier and faster, while making your file sizes as small as possible. If you incorporate these tips into your Web work, before you know it, you'll be earning more money, and then when you have enough money, you can buy cartons of cigarettes to bribe the guards. See, it all works out in the end.

ADDING MUSIC TO YOUR FLASH WEB GALLERY

In CS2 Adobe added two Flash-based templates you can use for your online Web Photo Gallery. Even cooler is the fact that you can now add a background music track to one of these Flash galleries. Just follow these steps: First find the MP3 audio track you want to use as your background music and rename the file as "useraudio.mp3". Then open your Photoshop CS2 application folder, navigate to Presets, and choose Web Photo Gallery. Inside that folder look for either Flash Gallery 1 or Flash Gallery 2. Depending on which gallery you chose within Photoshop, drag-and-drop your audio file into the corresponding folder. That's it! You've got background music.

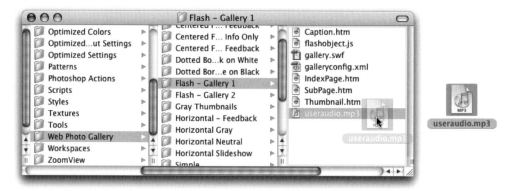

LOSE THOSE ANNOYING NUMBERS IN THE UPPER LEFT-HAND CORNER

We get more letters from people who ask us, "How do I get rid of that number in the top left-hand corner of my image?" This little puppy appears if you accidentally click on the Slice tool in the Toolbox. Even if you notice your error and immediately switch to another tool, it's too late. The "slice number" is already in place. To make it go away, go under the View menu, under Show, and choose Slices. Then try not to accidentally click on the Slice tool again. (Sorry, I felt like scolding somebody. You know, just for fun.)

NEED TO SHRINK THE FILE SIZE? USE TRANSPARENCY

Want a killer tip for squeezing even more size out of your GIF Web images? Make something transparent. That's right, if you can pick an area of your image to make transparent, your file size will drop like a rock. For example, if you're putting a logo over a white background and you can make the white area around the logo transparent, your file size will be significantly smaller, because the transparent areas are virtually ignored when determining file size, because, after all, there's nothing there.

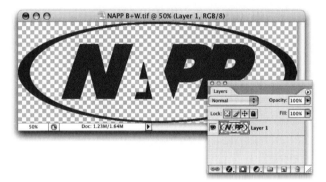

CROP IT EVEN CLOSER

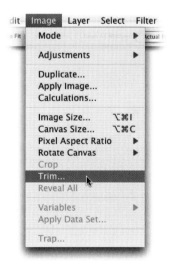

When you're designing graphics for the Web, you don't want even one extra pixel of unused space, because it adds to the overall file size of the image. Because of that, you want to crop your Web graphics as tightly as possible. Luckily for us (you, them, etc.), Photoshop CS2 can do it for you automatically. Just choose Trim from the Image menu, click OK in the dialog, and it will crop your Web graphic as tightly as possible for the smallest possible file size. It does this by looking at the pixel color in the upper left-hand corner of your image and cropping down until it hits another color. (*Note:* The Trim dialog also gives you the option to base the crop on the bottom right-hand corner pixel color or transparent areas.) This works especially well when creating type for the Web, because you'll often create it on a white background.

LET PHOTOSHOP MAKE THE FILE SIZE CALL

Oftentimes you have a target size you're trying to hit when creating Web graphics; for example, you're creating a Web banner and your file size limit is 32 K. If that's the case, and you know the target size, why not let Photoshop do all the work? Here's how: Under the File menu, go to Save for Web. In the Save for Web dialog, just to the right of the Settings pop-up menu, is a right-facing triangle. Click-and-hold it and when the pop-up menu appears, choose Optimize to File Size. In the dialog, enter the target file size you

need your graphic to be and click OK to have Photoshop optimize the graphic to fit your target file size. If it doesn't matter to you whether it's a GIF or JPEG, choose Auto Select GIF/JPEG and Photoshop will "make the call."

ZOOM OUT FOR SHARPER WEB IMAGES

This is a tip we use almost daily when we have to greatly reduce the size and/or resolution of an image. Sometimes when you make a drastic size/resolution change, it can really make the resulting image blurry, so what we do is simply zoom out on the image so that the window and image are at either 50% or 25% view. Then, we take a screen capture of our image window at the new smaller size. That way, the image still looks sharp, but it's much smaller when we open the screen capture in Photoshop. The

trick to making this work is using either a 50%, 25%, or 12.5% view size for making the capture. If you view the image at 66.7%, 33.3%, or 16.7%, the image won't be as crisp (because of the way Photoshop draws the image at those views).

IMAGEREADY FEATURE COMES TO PHOTOSHOP

One of our favorite little features from Adobe ImageReady has made its way into Photoshop—it's called Slices From Guides. What it does is slice your image (for the Web) where
your guides are positioned. To make use of this handy little number, just make your rulers
visible by pressing Command-R (PC: Control-R), drag out guides where you'd like your slices
applied, and then press the letter K to use the Slice tool. With the Slice tool selected, look
up in the Options Bar and you'll find a button called Slices From Guides. Click the button
and Photoshop will do the rest.

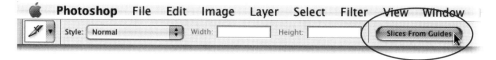

TWO EASY WAYS TO CREATE TRANSPARENCY

The most common
method for making a
background transparent
back in Photoshop 6.0
is still available to you in
Photoshop CS2, and that's
to go to the Layers palette
and simply delete the
Background layer. That's
it. This leaves only the
layers that were above the
Background layer (which
already have background
transparency). Now, there's
another easy way, and
that's to go to Photoshop's
Save for Web command,
switch to the Eyedropper
tool in the Save for Web's
Toolbox, and click on the background color you want to become transparent. Then, just below
the Color Table on the bottom right of the dialog, click on the first icon, which creates transparency from your selected color.

©ISTOCKPHOTO/MIKE BENTLEY

IMAGEREADY WINDOW SPEED TIP

If you're using Adobe Image-Ready (which comes installed with Photoshop as part of the package), by default the image window displays the original (un-optimized version) of your image. However, if you want to quickly view the optimized version, a 2-Up version (original and optimized side-by-side), or the 4-Up version (your original and three other optimized options), you can use the quick tip Command-Y (PC: Control-Y) to rotate through your four view choices. A big time saver.

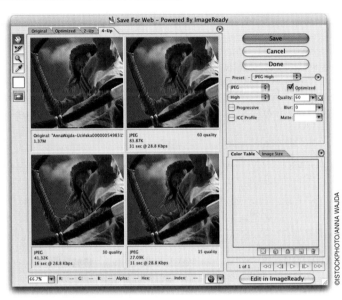

IF IT'S WEB SAFE, DON'T USE IT

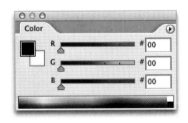

The one palette that we absolutely don't use at all anymore is the Web-safe Color palette (choose Web Color Sliders from the Color palette's flyout menu). Why? You don't need it—and it can make your file sizes significantly larger than necessary. The Web-safe colors were created back when most computer users had computers that could only display a maximum of 256 colors. Out of those 256, the "Web-safe" colors were the 216 colors that were the same on both Macintosh and Windows browsers. Even back then you could still use a non-Web-safe color, but it might dither to the next closest Web-safe color so the color might be off a bit. However, if you've ever looked at a row of monitors at the computer store, you'll notice the color is slightly different on every one, but that's another story. Luckily these days, you'd be hard-pressed to find anyone using such a lame computer that it only displays 256 colors. They haven't sold a computer like that for literally years.

⬤ ⬤ ⬤ CHANGE ONE PREFERENCE, SAVE A BUNDLE

If you're creating Web graphics with Photoshop and you're not using the Save for Web feature (which is perfectly fine not to do), make sure you go under the Photoshop menu (in Mac OS X), under Preferences, and choose File Handling (in Windows, Preferences can be found under the Edit menu). In the Image Previews pop-up, change the setting from Always Save to Never Save. Image Previews are those tiny thumbnail icons that are visible on your system. They look cute, but they take up big space—often accounting for 70% of your file size. Turn them off, and you'll save file size big time. (Save for Web does this automatically, so if you're using that feature, don't sweat it.)

 **GET THE REAL 100% VIEW**

When creating Web graphics, it's often important to view your graphic at the same size your audience will view it. To view your image at 100%, just double-click on the Zoom tool. If your image is too big when viewed at 100%, just zoom out until the view of your image is the size you'd like it to appear on the webpage (use the zoom-out shortcuts—click with the Zoom tool while holding the Option/Alt keys, etc.), then look in the lower-left corner of the image window and you'll see the percentage of zoom. Write that down, then go under the Image menu and choose Image Size. When the Image Size dialog appears, in the Height pop-up menu in the Pixel Dimensions section, choose Percent. Then enter the percentage amount you wrote down earlier. By default, Photoshop will enter the Width when you enter the Height setting to keep your image proportional (if not, make sure the Constrain Proportions checkbox is turned on at the bottom). Click OK and it resizes your image to the exact size you want it to appear on the webpage.

STYLE WARNING FOR WEB DESIGNERS

If you're designing Web graphics using Photoshop and ImageReady, you're probably spending a decent amount of time swapping back and forth between the two apps. The two programs share many of the same features and commands. However, they don't share custom styles that you've saved in Photoshop's Styles palette. So just be forewarned: If you create a custom style in Photoshop, don't expect to find that same style in ImageReady.

New Style

Name: MyOwnStyle

OK
Cancel

☑ Include Layer Effects
☐ Include Layer Blending Options

SPEND MORE TIME ANIMATING, LESS TIME CLICKING

If you're building Web animations in ImageReady, you don't have to keep clicking the tiny controls at the bottom of the Animations palette. Instead, navigate using these quick shortcuts: To play your animation, press Shift-Spacebar. To stop it, press Shift-Spacebar again. Press Option-Left Arrow (PC: Alt-Left Arrow) to go to the previous frame. Press Option-Right Arrow (PC: Alt-Right Arrow) to go to the next frame. To quickly jump back to the beginning of your animation, press Option-Shift-Left Arrow (PC: Alt-Shift-Left Arrow).

⬤ ⬤ ⬤ GETTING TO THE HEXADECIMAL CODE

As you may know, there are hexadecimal codes for the colors used in webpages. Not only does Photoshop know these hexadecimal codes, it can extract them from an image and let you paste them into your HTML code editor. First, press the letter I to switch to the Eyedropper tool, and then hold the Control key (PC: Right-click) and click on a color within your image. A contextual menu will appear where you can choose Copy Color as HTML. Now you can switch to your HTML editor and choose Paste to copy the HTML code into your app.

⬤ ⬤ ⬤ GET SUPER-CLEAN TYPE FOR THE WEB

If you've been faced with having to create small type on the Web (usually 12 points or fewer), you know the smaller you go, the

blurrier your type gets. That's because of the anti-aliasing that's automatically applied to the type, which works fine at larger sizes but tends to run together at smaller sizes, making your type look fuzzy. You can adjust the amount of aliasing (from the Options Bar), but here's a tip that many Web designers feel works even better: Once you get below 12 points, start adding positive tracking to your type (anywhere between 20 to 50 points) in the Character palette. This increases the amount of space between letters, and therefore, decreases the amount of blurriness. Increasing the space between your letters this way minimizes the effects of anti-aliasing and makes your type cleaner and more readable at smaller sizes. As a general rule—the smaller the type, the larger the tracking amount.

GOT A FOLDER FULL OF IMAGES FOR THE WEB? BATCH 'EM!

Do you have a whole folder of images that you're going to convert to Web graphics? If the images are somewhat similar, don't do them one at a time—automate the process using actions. Start by opening one image from the folder. Go to the Actions palette (under the Window menu) and click on the Create New Action icon. Give this action a name (something like Optimize as JPEGs) then go about the business of optimizing this one graphic into a JPEG for the Web. When you're done optimizing it, click the Stop button at the bottom of the Actions palette. Then go under the File menu, under Automate, and choose Batch. In this dialog, under Play, choose the name of the new action you just created. Under Source, choose the folder of images you want converted using that action, and under Destination, choose what you want to happen to those images after they're converted. Click OK, and Photoshop will convert that folder with absolutely blinding speed. This one tip can really change the way you work, especially if you create for print first, then repurpose for the Web afterward.

EXERCISING YOUR INFLUENCE ON GIFS

This is an old trick we use to influence how Photoshop builds its color table when creating GIF images. We put a selection around the area of the image that's most important to us (for example, if we had a product shot, we'd put a selection around it), then we'd convert to Indexed Color (by choosing it from the Mode submenu under the Image menu). Photoshop will look at the colors contained in your selection and build the Indexed Color Table giving preference to those colors. It's another slick way to use less colors, creating a smaller file, but with a better-looking image.

READ THE WEB COLOR ONSCREEN

Want to know the hexadecimal Web color values of any color in your image? The Info palette can tell you instantly. Go under the Window menu and choose Info. In the Info palette, click on the little Eyedropper icon next to the CMYK readout and a pop-up menu appears. Choose Web Color, and you'll get the hexadecimal readouts right in the palette.

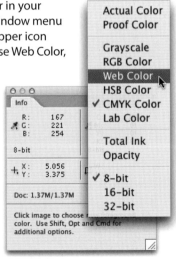

IMAGEREADY'S SUPERCHARGED EYEDROPPER

In previous versions of Photoshop, you could only use the Eyedropper tool to sample a color from other open images in Photoshop, but for some reason, ImageReady had a supercharged Eyedropper. If you clicked the mouse button within your image and held it down, you could leave your image window and sample colors from, well… just about anything—including your computer desktop or any other open application. Freaky! Fortunately, Adobe finally added this same power to Photoshop's Eyedropper tool.

IMAGEREADY'S AUTO TILE MAKER

ImageReady has a built-in tool for creating seamless backgrounds. It's called Tile Maker and it's found under the Filter menu, under Other. It brings up a dialog where you can choose how much you want to blend the edges of your images (the default setting of 10 percent works fairly well for most images), but you can increase it if it doesn't look smooth enough to you.

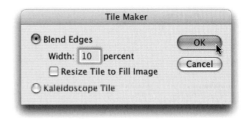

MAKE SURE YOU SEE IT THE SAME WAY THEY SEE IT

If you're designing Web graphics on a Macintosh, you can be sure they're going to be viewed by lots of people using a PC, and vice versa. A design problem arises because the monitors on Macs and on PCs display with different levels of brightness. For example, if you design Web graphics on a Macintosh, they'll look more than 10% darker when viewed on a PC using Windows. Photoshop will let you see an approximation of how those graphics will look when viewed on a PC. Here's how: Choose Save for Web

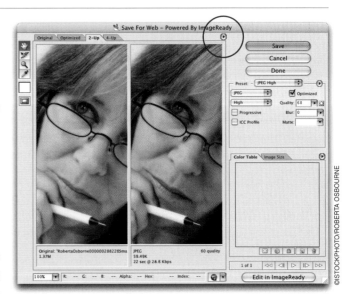

from the File menu. Then, at the top right of the preview window you'll see a pop-up menu called the Preview Menu. From that menu, choose Standard Windows Color to get a preview of how your currently opened graphic will look when viewed on a standard Windows monitor. Windows designers can do the same thing and view how their Web graphics will look when viewed on a Mac (they'll look lighter). Knowing how your graphics will look on each platform will help you find a happy middle ground that looks good on both.

DON'T LOAD THAT BOGUS SLICE!

If you're slicing images for the Web in Photoshop (using the Slice tool), here's a tip to save even more space. If you have a slice in your image that's going to be the same color as your background (for example, you've got a solid white slice going on a solid white background), you can save file size by having that slice load no image at all. Sound like a plan? (I thought you'd like that.) Here's how to do it: Once your slice is in place, make it active (using the Slice Select tool), and then double-click within the selection to get the Slice Options dialog. In the Slice Type pop-up menu, choose No Image and click OK. That way, when Photoshop generates its HTML for the page, there will be no image in that spot, just the white background showing through, giving you a faster loading webpage. Pretty sweet!

USE LAYER-BASED SLICES

If you're getting ready to slice an image for the Web and you still have your layers intact, don't flatten that image before you slice. Instead, let Photoshop create the (layer-based) slices for you. There are two main advantages: (1) it's easier. You don't have to drag out slices—Photoshop does it automatically, perfectly slicing at the size of your layer. But even better is (2), when you create a layer-based slice, you can move the layer and (get this) Photoshop will automatically adjust all the slices to accommodate your move, and it will create a new slice for your layer as well. If you slice manually and move your layer—you're out of luck—the old slice stays right where it was. Plus, creating a layer-based slice couldn't be easier. Click on the layer you want to slice, then go under the Layer menu and choose New Layer Based Slice—Photoshop does the rest.

⬤ ⬤ ⬤ BLUR THAT JPEG AND SHRINK IT DOWN

Here's a cool tip for when you're creating JPEG images. This tip doesn't work for all images, but can really come in handy for others. The tip is this: Because of the way JPEG compression works, if you can slightly blur your image, the file size will be smaller. You could just add a Gaussian Blur, or you could blur the image directly from the Save for Web dialog by entering a number in the Blur field. However, you're usually better off putting a selection around the important areas of your image, then inverting the selection (by choosing Inverse from the Select menu) and blurring just the background. That way, the important parts stay sharp, and the noncritical areas become more compressed.

Index

COLOPHON

The book was produced by the author and design team using all Macintosh computers, including a Power Mac G5 1.8-GHz, a Power Mac G5 Dual Processor 1.8-GHz, a Power Mac G5 Dual Processor 2-GHz, a Power Mac G4 Dual Processor 1.25-MHz. We use LaCie, Sony, and Apple Studio Display monitors.

Page layout was done using Adobe InDesign CS. We use a Mac OS X server, and burn our CDs to our CPU's internal Sony DVD RW DW-U10A.

The headers for each technique are set in Adobe Myriad Pro Semibold at 11 points on 12.5 leading, with the Horizontal Scaling set to 100%. Body copy is set using Adobe Myriad Pro Regular at 9.5 points on 11.5 leading, with the Horizontal Scaling set to 100%.

Screen captures were made with Snapz Pro X and were placed and sized within Adobe InDesign CS. The book was output at 150 line screen, and all in-house printing was done using a Tektronix Phaser 7700 by Xerox.

ADDITIONAL RESOURCES

ScottKelbyBooks.com
For information on Scott's other Macintosh and graphics-related books, visit his book site. For background info on Scott, visit www.scottkelby.com.

http://www.scottkelbybooks.com

Layers Magazine
Layers—The How-To Magazine for Everything Adobe—is the foremost authority on Adobe's design, digital video, digital photography, and education applications. Each issue features timely product news, plus the quick tips, hidden shortcuts, and step-by-step tutorials for working in today's digital market. America's top-selling computer book author for 2004, Scott Kelby is editor-in-chief of *Layers*.

www.layersmagazine.com

National Association of Photoshop Professionals (NAPP)
The industry trade association for Adobe® Photoshop® users and the world's leading resource for Photoshop training, education, and news.

http://www.photoshopuser.com

KW Computer Training Videos
Scott Kelby is featured in a series of Photoshop training DVDs, each on a particular Photoshop topic, available from KW Computer Training. Visit the website or call 813-433-5000 for orders or more information.

http://www.photoshopvideos.com

Photoshop Down & Dirty Tricks
Scott is also author of the best-selling book *Photoshop CS Down & Dirty Tricks*, and the book's companion website has all the info on the book, which is available at bookstores around the country.

http://www.scottkelbybooks.com

Adobe Photoshop Seminar Tour
See Scott live at the Adobe Photoshop Seminar Tour, the nation's most popular Photoshop seminars. For upcoming tour dates and class schedules, visit the tour website.

http://www.photoshopseminars.com

Photoshop World
The convention for Adobe Photoshop users has now become the largest Photoshop-only event in the world. Scott Kelby is technical chair and education director for the event, as well as one of the instructors.

http://www.photoshopworld.com

The Photoshop CS2 Book for Digital Photographers
This book cuts through the bull and shows you step by step the exact techniques used by today's cutting-edge digital photographers, and it shows you which settings to use, when to use them, and why.

http://www.scottkelbybooks.com

Photoshop Hall of Fame
Created to honor and recognize those individuals whose contributions to the art and business of Adobe Photoshop have had a major impact on the application or the Photoshop community itself.

http://www.photoshophalloffame.com